The Oprah Winfrey Show

Reflections on an American Legacy

The Oprah Winfrey Show

Reflections on an American Legacy

By Deborah Davis
Abrams, New York

The Making of a Legacy   6

Phenomenal Maya Angelou   24

Introduction   26

A Forum for Women   29   Soul Searching   119
Gloria Steinem   Mark Nepo
Maria Shriver   Marianne Williamson
                                     Dr. Phil McGraw

Star Power   49   In Good Health   141
John Travolta   Bob Greene
Diane von Furstenberg   Dr. Mehmet Oz
Julia Roberts .

Embracing Equality   75   Here's to Books   157
Stanley Crouch   Toni Morrison
Ellen DeGeneres   Elie Wiesel
Henry Louis Gates, Jr.
                                     Moving the Needle   177
Giving Back   97   Phil Donahue
Nicholas Kristof   Roger Ebert
Bono
Nelson Mandela   The Farewell Season   199
                                     Sidney Poitier

The End of an Era   220

Notes, Credits & Acknowledgments   238

||SEG 1 INTRO||

comment on show open-walk out through LED

THERE ARE NO WORDS TO MATCH THIS
MOMENT.

EVERY WORD I'VE EVER SPOKEN FROM
THIS STAGE OF THE OPRAH SHOW FOR
4,561 DAYS OF MY LIFE IS WHAT THIS
MOMENT IS ALL ABOUT

YESTERDAY YOU HEARD THE
LEGENDARY ARETHA FRANKLIN SING
WHAT HAS BEEN & MY LIFE CONSTANT THEME
SONG: "AMAZING GRACE"

Phenomenal
Maya Angelou

There's no straight line from Kosciusko, Mississippi, to Paris, France, or to London, England, or to, for that matter, Chicago, Illinois. The fact is that Oprah Winfrey reaches all those places with her irresistible personality and charm.

Her journey has been, and still is, complicated. She was born poor in a poverty-stricken village in Mississippi. She was born Black in an era and an area where racism was the order of the day and was to be expected and legally accepted.

Fortunately, before she reached her teens, she had heard and believed the lyrics of an old gospel that advised, "Don't you let nobody turn you round, turn you round, turn you round."

She decided that she would not allow anyone or any group to reduce her humanity.

Oprah began to read in the library of the Black school in Kosciusko, Mississippi. She drank down novels as if they contained the sweet iced tea of southern summers. She met White children in the pages who were worlds apart from the mean White youngsters who teased her and called her vulgar names in the dirt roads of her hometown. She read and memorized the poetry of the great African American poets Langston Hughes and Paul Laurence Dunbar. Their lines, filled with self-respect, had an enormous impact on the young Winfrey. The poets exclaimed that Black was not only beautiful, but also exquisite. Langston Hughes's "Harlem Sweeties" told her that her complexion was perfect, and the poem strengthened her resolve to grow beyond the confines of negativity.

> Have you dug the spill
> Of Sugar Hill?
> Cast your gims
> On this sepia thrill:
> Brown sugar lassie,
> Caramel treat,
> Honey-gold baby
> Sweet enough to eat.
>
>   * * *
>
> So if you want to know beauty's
> Rainbow-sweet thrill,
> Stroll down luscious,
> Delicious, fine Sugar Hill.

Oprah, like any other southern-born Black child, desperately needed the assurance that African Americans were worthy of praise and appreciation. She found that assurance in James Weldon Johnson's song, "Lift Every Voice and Sing," known as the African American National Anthem.

> Lift every voice and sing,
> Till earth and heaven ring,
> Ring with the harmonies of Liberty;
> Let our rejoicing rise
> High as the listening skies,
> Let it resound loud as the rolling sea.
> Sing a song full of the faith that the dark past has taught us,
> Sing a song full of the hope that the present has brought us;
> Facing the rising sun of our new day begun.
> Let us march on till victory is won.

The climate in Kosciusko was heavy with the idea that White was always right and White had might and that Black should always get back, get back. Oprah decided that she would not indulge any man-made hindrance between human beings constructed for someone else's convenience and at someone else's whim.

The question was: How could a Black girl born into such a negative climate escape this crippling environment and become one of the most powerful voices in the world?

Oprah used her deeply felt religion to combat all the offensive strikes against her. She believed that she was a child of God and took sincerely the words of a nineteenth-century hymn writer:

> My Father is rich in houses and lands,
> He holdeth the wealth of the world in His hands!
> Of rubies and diamonds, of silver and gold,
> His coffers are filled, He has riches untold.
>
> I'm a child of the King.
> A child of the King:
> With Jesus my Savior,
> I'm a child of the King.

She began to recite in her grandmother's church, and the older church members commended her, bragged about her, and said she was very good.

When Oprah Winfrey left Mississippi and later went to live with her father in Tennessee, she found herself less restricted, less hemmed in by racism.

Conversations in her father's barbershop were driven by political and social issues. Winfrey bloomed. When she entered Tennessee State University, she was convinced of a belief she had held secretly and that belief was: She was, after all, very intelligent.

Oprah Winfrey was given not only a fine brain but also enormous energy. Her ambitions had not focused on any desire, save to be the best she could be.

When I was told of this book and informed that a number of people would write about Oprah Winfrey and possibly describe her, I was reminded of an ancient Indian folktale about a group of blind people who were asked to describe a super-size elephant.

One person was taken to the elephant's side. He used both hands to feel the rough skin of the animal. He exclaimed, "I know what an elephant is. He is a hairy wall."

The second person was given the wiggly tail, and he shouted, "An elephant is a very excited snake."

A third person was guided to the trunk, and he said, "I know an elephant is a tree." Each person found another portion of the elephant to describe.

Ms. Oprah Winfrey is much more complex than an elephant or even a herd of elephants. These writers (I include myself) who have attempted to describe Oprah are not blind. So I am sure this book will offer many facts. Since I know that facts can often obscure the truth, I can tell you one truth about Oprah Winfrey that I have learned in our friendship over twenty-five years.

Oprah Winfrey is a child of God and a citizen of the world. Phenomenally.

> Now you understand
> Just why my head's not bowed.
> I don't shout or jump about
> Or have to talk real loud.
> When you see me passing,
> It ought to make you proud.
> I say,
> It's in the click of my heels.
> The bend of my hair,
> The palms of my hands.
> The need for my care.
> 'Cause I'm a woman
> Phenomenally.
> Phenomenal woman,
> That's Oprah.

Introduction

The last episode of *The Oprah Winfrey Show* aired on May 25, 2011, prompting Oprah enthusiasts to fondly recall their favorite moments—a revealing interview, a life-changing lesson, a good read, a provocative debate, an emotionally charged glimpse into tragedy or natural disaster, or a makeover of the mind or body, to name a few. It was a sad time for dedicated viewers who had difficulty envisioning life without Oprah (in their minds, the woman and the show were one and the same). But, the show's end also sparked a lively debate on an issue that would now preoccupy fans and critics alike: After 4,561 episodes, nearly 30,000 guests, and 1.3 million audience members, what did it all mean? What was the true legacy of *The Oprah Winfrey Show*?

Wellness was one thought: Oprah encouraged America to get healthy and assembled a dream team of doctors and experts to lead the way. Literacy was another: Oprah propelled books to the center of the culture and turned reading into a national pastime akin in popularity to baseball. And, speaking of culture, she was one of the most influential figures in the entertainment business and became the leading arbiter of "hot" and "not." Oprah carried the banner for women, advocated equality for all, and extolled the virtues of philanthropy. She emphasized the importance of spirituality and personal growth in an age when people rarely looked within. And she transformed the media by turning talk into action, and action into results.

The Oprah Winfrey Show was such a fundamental part of the American experience that references to it turn up everywhere. In May 1993, the word "Oprah" became a verb, defined by *Details* magazine as meaning "to engage in persistent, intimate questioning with the aim of obtaining a confession." The example cited was something along the lines of "I wasn't going to tell her. . . but she Oprahed it out of me."

The show's power to confer success on individuals and products lives in legend. Even with all the publicity surrounding the show's end, people continue to offer the not-so-helpful suggestion "You should go on *Oprah*" when there is something to promote, despite the fact that, sadly, it is no longer a possibility. No one has emerged to take her place.

A Chicago woman who was trying to get excused from jury duty argued that she couldn't serve because she had once-in-a-lifetime tickets to a final taping of *The Oprah Winfrey Show*. Though she was a potential pick for a high-profile case—the retrial of former Illinois governor Rod Blagojevich—both the prosecution and the defense acknowledged the validity of her excuse. "It's the last year [of Oprah's show], Judge," the prosecutor explained, and the woman was released from her obligation.

Left: Oprah's personal journal entry from September 8, 1986, the day of her first show.

Right: Oprah and an audience member during the first show, September 8, 1986.

Left: Oprah announces that she is ending *The Oprah Winfrey Show* after the twenty-fifth season, November 20, 2009.

Right: Oprah waves good-bye to the studio audience and viewers around the world as she walks off the stage of *The Oprah Winfrey Show* for the last time, May 25, 2011.

On a more serious note, one of the most exhaustive examinations of Oprah Winfrey's legacy was mounted by no less an authority than the Harvard Business School. In 2005, Oprah was the subject of one of the school's hallmark case studies. "I've always been interested in individuals whose experience summarizes large lessons for our moment. . . . What is it about Oprah that business leaders can learn from in the twenty-first century?" asked Nancy F. Koehn, a professor in the MBA program. The resulting study explored Oprah's phenomenal success as an entrepreneur, businesswoman, and brand.

It also addressed her unique ability to connect with people emotionally. Koehn described a male MBA student with a background in finance (certainly not a typical fan) "raising his hand in class and saying, 'My mom got divorced several years ago, and I have to tell you that Oprah's been like a guru to her.' . . . He spoke with great respect about Oprah because he had watched his mother find so much inspiration in Oprah's television show."

That student's mother, along with millions of other viewers, helped to build and shape the legacy. They sent their friend Oprah an average of twenty-five thousand letters and emails a week. "Dear Oprah, I have always wanted to thank you for saving my life"; "Dear Oprah, I watched your show and I was inspired"; "Dear Oprah, God bless you for having the courage to speak to the child molesters face-to-face"; "Dear Oprah, I thought all husbands hit their wives." When they spoke, Oprah listened, became their voice, and was heard far beyond the confines of television. "Oprah is bigger than TV," suggested journalist Rob Sheffield in *Rolling Stone*. "In fact, future generations may remember TV as 'the thing Oprah was on,' the way we mostly remember iambic pentameter as Shakespeare's format."

What was the legacy of *The Oprah Winfrey Show*? Like the dots in a pointillist painting by French master Georges Seurat, the individual episodes combined to make a powerful whole, a colorful canvas full of subjects, people, stories, ideas, and perspectives. Whenever Oprah introduced us to a person we never met, a pain we never felt, a thought we never considered, a possibility we never imagined, or a question we never asked, we evolved, and the world evolved with us. Looking back—and looking forward—the show, and the woman who gave it its name, have had a profound and unprecedented impact on life and the way we live it.

A Forum for Women

"Our deepest fear is not that we are inadequate. Our deepest fear is that we are powerful beyond measure."

–Marianne Williamson

Oprah Winfrey grew to become an enduring symbol of life's possibilities, proof that closed doors, glass ceilings, racial barriers, and other obstacles couldn't keep an "I can do it" woman down.

The Oprah Winfrey Show had a twenty-five-year love affair with its audience, most of whom were women—young, old, and somewhere in between; rich, poor, and just getting by; fat, thin, and on a diet; happy, sad, and in treatment; married, single, and "it's complicated." *All* kinds of women, from all walks of life, moved closer to the electronic campfire that was *Oprah* to watch, to listen, to learn, and to be honored for who they were, and who they could be. "Oprah is to women what sports is to men," a media executive wisely observed.

When the show debuted in 1986, mostly "housewives" watched daytime television, and long before they became colorfully "desperate," they were perceived as a conventional and even complacent audience. But when Oprah Winfrey looked into the faces in her studio—and considered the viewers at home—she saw modern-day Sleeping Beauties, women who were ready to be awakened, enlightened, empowered, and transformed. And when these women looked back at Oprah, they recognized the friend, mother, sister, teacher, and advocate who could jump-start their evolution—their *revolution* of self-development and growth.

Oprah Winfrey grew to become an enduring symbol of life's possibilities, proof that closed doors, glass ceilings, racial barriers, and other obstacles couldn't keep an "I can do it" woman down. Her show's mission was to provide other women with the necessary tools to help *them* make can-do choices in their own lives. Oprah was their trusted companion and mentor on that journey, influencing "the way women think, talk, eat, study, shop, exercise, and lead." Whether conducting an emotionally charged interview with troubled superstar Whitney Houston, or exploring the feelings of an overwhelmed young mother, Oprah used their stories to create a comprehensive living handbook for women, with subjects ranging from anorexia to Zen meditation. Problems—and their solutions—varied over time, but Oprah's message was constant: What's on *your* mind is on *my* mind, and no matter what your problem is, or how horrible you imagine it to be, you are not alone.

Although women are considered humanity's caretakers, they are notoriously bad at taking care of themselves. Used to being described as hypochondriacs, or dismissed

Left: Whitney Houston and Oprah at the taping of their two-part interview, September 14 and 15, 2009.

Right: Dr. Christiane Northrup discusses how menopause can heal the mind, body, and spirit, March 7, 2001.

as having "female trouble" (a term covering anything remotely hormonal), women typically ignored their own health and wellness problems because they were busy, ill-informed, or sometimes ashamed to discuss subjects they considered overly personal or taboo. *The Oprah Winfrey Show* addressed their concerns and invited smart, sympathetic experts to offer guidance.

Weight was one of *Oprah*'s most enduring topics. Oprah famously shared her diet successes and failures on the show, but she also invited other women to join the conversation. Eventually, they felt comfortable discussing a subject that most women considered painful and humiliating. On an episode titled "Women's Love Affair with Food," a group of ordinary women explored their feelings about overeating. What they said wasn't as important as the fact that Oprah enabled them to feel secure enough to say it. On *The Oprah Winfrey Show*, weight loss wasn't a competition, with thinner women emerging as the winners; it was the starting point for an important and ongoing discussion about deeper issues, such as self-esteem, depression, and fear of abandonment.

Oprah routinely tackled health-related issues that were important to women, including stress ("If I could have me a wife it would be the most wonderful thing," said one overworked mom), and sex (the mysteries of the "vajajay," as Oprah called it, and the pursuit of the elusive orgasm). Menopause, a topic once confined to gatherings of proverbial "old wives," came out into the light on the show, and with an entirely new spin. Oprah said, "We just need a shift in our perception, and I'm ready to shift." According to Dr. Christiane Northrup, author of *The Wisdom of Menopause,* the "Big M" did not have to represent the end of life as women knew it. It could be a time of rebirth. Attend to the physical changes with proper diet (low consumption of alcohol, caffeine, sugar, and carbohydrates) and exercise, and open the mind to the new experiences that arise after the childbearing years. That was Dr. Northrup's prescription for a graceful and productive menopause, and women listened.

As Oprah pointed out, menopause was not a threat. But she did name "The Number One Killer of Women" on a show that aired in 2005. This is "the mother of all wake-up

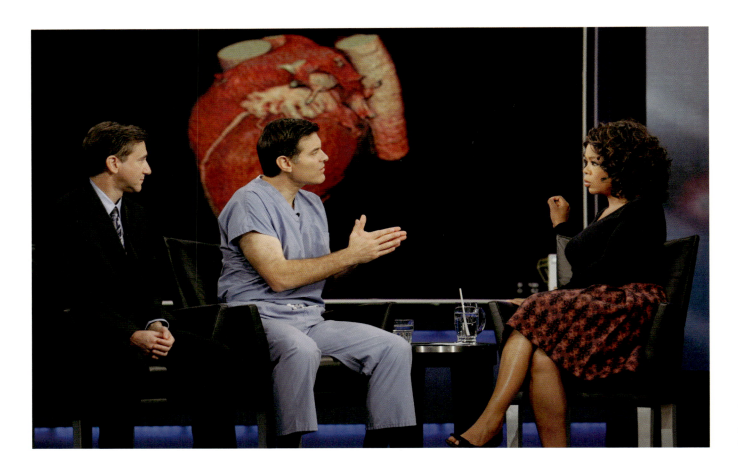

Dr. Andrew Rosenson, Dr. Mehmet Oz, and Oprah talk about heart health for women, October 19, 2005.

calls," she said. "One out of two [women] will die of this. It could be you." She was talking about cardiovascular disease, which kills more women than breast cancer each year and, in fact, kills more women than all other cancers combined. Dr. Oz showed the difference between healthy and unhealthy hearts, and educated women about tests, such as the CT scan, that could identify plaque in their arteries. Oprah urged viewers not to be afraid of test results, but to see information as power in *all* aspects of their lives.

Information presented on the show "How to Protect Yourself from an Attacker" actually did save lives. "At least one of the millions of you watching this show today, you're going to remember something that you saw on this show today in a crucial, critical moment and it is going to save your life," Oprah said prophetically when the episode aired in 1991. Women who had been the victims of violent crimes demonstrated the self-defense skills they learned after they were attacked. "This has changed my life," said a woman who, after she was gang-raped at the age of fourteen, realized that she had to learn how to protect herself so she wouldn't feel like a victim.

Later in the show, Oprah introduced Sanford Strong, who served twenty years with the San Diego Police Department.

Oprah also emphasized the importance of intuition in assessing danger. If something seems wrong, it probably is wrong.

Top: Erin Garrity defending herself against male "attackers," August 14, 1991.

Bottom: Sanford Strong, veteran San Diego detective, acts out the role of an attacker to make a crucial point about the importance of preparedness, August 14, 1991.

He shared his most important strategy for dealing with an attacker: "Rule number one—and frankly, it's probably, in my opinion, the most important: Never allow them to take you anywhere else. Never." Because crime scene number two is going to be isolated, you won't choose it, you'll be the focus of the crime." As Oprah predicted, his words had a tremendous impact on the women watching the show. "Never let them take you to a second location" became a lifesaving mantra for women who found themselves in dangerous situations.

A woman who survived an attack in Alabama wrote, "I was not an everyday watcher of *Oprah*, but I did happen to see one program about self-defense. The main thing I learned was to never, never, never get into a car to be taken to a second location. I knew that if I let him put me into the car, I would never get out of it alive." She later learned that her assailant may have abducted and killed a woman just two days after he assaulted her. A woman who was carjacked said that she recalled the key tip from *The Oprah Winfrey Show*—don't allow yourself to be taken to a second location—and leapt from the moving car to escape an attacker. Happily, she lived to tell the tale. Actress Gabrielle Union recalled being surprised by a rapist when she was nineteen, and all she could think about was the "no second location" rule she heard on *Oprah*. One lesson, effectively delivered, saved many, many lives.

Oprah also emphasized the importance of intuition in assessing danger. If something seems wrong, it probably is wrong, she advised. Too often, people fail to listen to what security expert Gavin de Becker called the "gift of fear," the inner voice that signals trouble. A woman had a funny feeling that someone was in her apartment when she wasn't there, and caught a stalker on a hidden camera. Another woman had the sense that the "Good Samaritan" helping her with her groceries was "off," but ignored her feeling and he followed her into her apartment and raped her. A daughter had second thoughts about her elderly father's nurse, and discovered she was beating him. Animals follow their intuition by running away from danger; humans—especially women—must learn to trust their inner voice and do the same.

Gloria Steinem

OPRAH!

Has Oprah Winfrey helped the female half of the world? That doesn't seem too big a question to ask about a woman who has been a daily presence on every continent and in 150 countries for a quarter of a century. Her television show became a real and rare example of a spontaneous democracy in which people from every walk of life were invited to talk honestly and were listened to with empathy and respect. They also learned to respect the authority of a woman of color who might otherwise have symbolized the largest group in the world with the least power. By inviting honesty from the famous and the obscure alike—and by focusing on understanding instead of blaming—she linked people rather than ranking them; something even democracies haven't figured out how to do.

With the wisdom of hindsight, I would say that Oprah created a global campfire that filled our timeless need to gather in a circle, listen to and learn from the stories of others, and tell our own—to have both uniqueness and community. Because most of the media was devoted to ranking people, to reporting statistics but not stories and problems but not solutions—especially given the culturally masculine notion that only conflict is news—*The Oprah Winfrey Show* was water in the desert. No wonder it became one of the most popular and longest-running television shows in history.

Though this campfire changed consciousness by its form alone, Oprah kept adding surprises to its content. She talked with everyone from survivors of childhood sexual abuse (which she herself was) to candidates for the U.S. presidency (which some suggested she could ultimately become); from sex-trafficked girls to men in prison for crimes against women; from veterans of street and military wars to survivors of family violence that normalizes all other violence. Each person became a teacher from whom Oprah learned. And we learned, too.

As someone who was traveling and listening to women during all those years—here and also in countries as different as South Africa and South Korea—I grew to believe that historians should recognize Oprah as a global influence. She was a leader in the most powerful way: by example. Women knew she had survived being motherless, poor, sexually abused; growing up in a racist and sexist culture; and her own self-doubt—all by taking orders from no one and living on books and hope. They also understood that, having longed for the power to decide her own life, she would defend that right for others. For instance, even when she talked about the death of her new-born after an unwanted pregnancy in her early teens, she dared to call it her "second chance at life." She also lived openly with a long-term male partner and never pretended she wanted marriage or motherhood. Yet as her show became a global forum for those experiences, I never saw a guest who said or implied that Oprah couldn't empathize and understand.

Just as she invited others to share enthusiasms, she shared her own. Her love of books made her describe them and interview authors in a way that intrigued viewers, created book clubs, and attracted millions more readers to worthwhile literature. From music to food and style, she introduced her audiences to whatever she loved. That included movies, television series, and plays that she publicized on her show or acted in and produced herself. Always honest about her long struggles with weight and body image, Oprah made it her goal to be healthy and kick her food addiction, not to be fashion-ably emaciated; therefore, she didn't spread the obsession with thinness. On the contrary, she became an influential example of a beautiful woman who was not thin. By introducing gay and lesbian guests who viewers grew to trust on everything from creating a home to understanding their gay children, she changed opinions on gay rights and marriage equality. And by becoming a philanthropist on a global scale, she inspired her viewers to give, too, and showed them important causes and ways to support them.

From listening to women talk about Oprah, I know she's been an inspiration on the touchy subject of money in other ways. First, she kept her credibility by refusing to profit from the countless books and products she personally recommended. Second, she became a self-made woman and entrepreneur whose personal worth reached $1 billion—something that made women proud of her for doing it on her own. Third, she never apologized for her success. Though the world tries to make women feel guilty and "unfeminine" for having power—so we'll remain without it—she enjoyed a good life of houses and travel and birthday parties while also supporting good causes, from her Leadership Academy for Girls in South Africa to reconstructing the Gulf Coast here in the United States. She performed the miracle of enjoying earned power while also using it well.

All this was not without punishment. After 9/11, Oprah created a series of thoughtful shows, including "Is War the Only Answer?" As she said, "I've never received more hate mail, like 'go back to Africa' hate mail." When an expert guest explained that mad cow disease was causing dementia in humans, Oprah said she wouldn't eat another burger. The beef industry charged her with "food disparagement," sued her for $10 million and created such sexist bumper stickers as THE ONLY MAD COW IN AMERICA IS OPRAH. At the opposite end of the political spectrum, some black activists grew suspicious of her popularity with white viewers and compared her to Aunt Jemima and Mammy. When she endorsed Barack Obama, protests grew so loud that I, who never would have thought Oprah needed my defense, found myself writing her a supportive letter and defending her on television. In the so-called serious press, she has continued to be ridiculed as the "Queen of Confessional TV," and even her success has been decried as the "Oprah-fication of the media."

Given the light cast by her global campfire, all I can say is: If only.

Perhaps her sin for her detractors is the same as her virtue for supporters: Oprah has inspired change from the bottom up and has become trusted and loved by remaining her authentic self.

In the same way that testifying in black churches sparked the civil rights movement, that "speaking-bitterness" circles began the Chinese revolution, and that consciousness-raising groups gave birth to this wave of feminism, ripples from twenty-five years of *The Oprah Winfrey Show* will keep rocking many boats. She proved once again that a circle is the strongest form in nature.

As Alice Walker wrote in her poem "We Alone":

This could be our revolution:
To love what is plentiful

as much as
what's scarce.

The Oprah Winfrey Show recognized that matters of the heart were of primary importance to women because they always seemed to be navigating the complicated waters of romantic relationships. In fact, "How to Marry the Man/Woman of Your Choice" was the subject of Oprah's very first show. Over the years, there were episodes about matchmaking, "'I Love You' Surprises," good guys, and great relationships. But like Leo Tolstoy, who observed in his classic novel Anna Karenina that "Happy families are all alike; every unhappy family is unhappy in its own way," Oprah realized that sensitively told stories about relationships-gone-wrong could serve as illuminating parables: Women had the opportunity to learn from other women's mistakes.

The show "I Killed My Ex and His Wife" explored the sad case of Betty Broderick, a woman serving thirty-two years to life in prison for committing a crime of passion. Broderick was the classic storybook wife who happily put her husband through medical and law school. They seemed to lead a charmed life together, until one day, without warning, he left her for his twenty-two-year-old assistant. Broderick had dedicated her entire life to her husband, but now he didn't want her. She didn't know what else to do, so she drove to his house and shot him, also killing his new wife, her younger replacement.

Oprah said that she learned something significant when she interviewed Betty Broderick. She was a woman who seemed to have everything, but had nothing because she was not in control of her own life. Broderick felt so worthless that the only way she believed she could get her ex-husband to listen to her was with a gun. Instead of evaluating her innocence or guilt, the show explored the initial mistakes that led Broderick to her terrible fate. In the beginning, when she surrendered her entire identity to her marriage, she lost what was most important in life: herself.

Like Broderick, Bridget's marriage started out as a fantasy. A successful businesswoman who fell hard for a charming Hollywood executive, she envisioned a future of happily-ever-after. But when she and her husband became ill after their honeymoon, she consulted his

Oprah realized that sensitively told stories about relationships-gone-wrong could serve as illuminating parables: Women had the opportunity to learn from other women's mistakes.

Gavin de Becker, Nicole, and Oprah on how the "gift of fear" can save your life, January 29, 2008.

doctor and was told that she was HIV positive *and* that she had infected her husband. Bridget experienced terrible feelings of guilt and remorse. Her whole life changed, until she realized that her husband was the one with the guilty secret. He was, and had been, actively engaged in surreptitious sexual relationships with other men—living on the "down low," so to speak. It was *his* lifestyle, not hers, that had destroyed them. Why was she so willing to believe that it was her fault?

Bridget, and unsuspecting women like her, were at risk, but didn't even know it. "This hidden culture of men living a dangerous lie has ruined lives," Oprah said on the show "Why She Sued Her Husband for $12 Million and Won." "It's broken up families and put so many women at risk." Oprah exposed the threat so that other women would be aware that it could touch *their* lives.

Whitney Houston's relationship with her husband, Bobby Brown, was headline news in every tabloid. But it wasn't until she opened up to Oprah in a dramatic two-part interview that she faced the tough questions about her turbulent marriage. "You were the first black princess," Oprah admonished, ". . . with a voice that's a national treasure, like nobody

else living at this time, and you're trying to pull yourself down." Houston's answers, candidly chronicling years of physical and emotional abuse, provided a cautionary tale for anyone locked into a destructive, codependent relationship.

The Oprah Winfrey Show also applied a no-holds-barred approach to the subject of motherhood. With Oprah, women did not have to pretend to love absolutely every aspect of this difficult, and often overwhelming, job. She gave mothers permission to feel exhausted, to have doubts, to question their dedication. More importantly, her show gave them a forum where they could express these conflicted emotions and, by sharing, learn from each other.

The topic of one show was "What Your Mother Never Told You About Motherhood." New mothers discussed the myths commonly associated with motherhood, explaining that the realities were very different from their expectations. A good deal of the time, they were tired and unfulfilled instead of being beatific madonnas. And, as one woman pointed out, "None of us have had the courage to stand and put our hands up and say, 'You know what? This sucks

Bridget, who says she contracted HIV from her husband's secret life "on the down low," October 7, 2010.

80 percent of the time.'" Motherhood also had an effect on sex. One wife confessed that after she puts the baby to bed, she feels like putting up a sign that says "closed."

Big mistake, according to author Ayelet Waldman, who raised eyebrows when she appeared on the show "A Mother's Controversial Confession." Waldman had said in a *New York Times* article that she loved her husband *more* than her children. In the same piece, the mother of four asserted that she was the "only woman in Mommy & Me who seems to be getting any." She stood by those sentiments on *Oprah*, arguing that women should not get lost in motherhood; they had to hold on to *themselves*. Oprah found Waldman's comments intriguing, especially the part about her sizzling sex life. "I have to say, you are the only woman I've ever heard say this," Oprah told her controversial guest. "I talk to women for a living . . . and all I ever hear is how women are sick of having sex . . . they're so tired. 'I love my husband, but I could care less if I ever had sex again,' they say."

Sex, especially in the "Mommy & Me" context, was a fairly lighthearted subject. But many new mothers faced a problem that was extremely serious, widely misunderstood, and had tragic consequences. Singer Marie Osmond introduced the topic to Oprah's audience in 1999, when she talked about her severe depression after giving birth to her seventh child. She felt sad and confused, and had trouble getting through the day. The simplest decisions, selecting panty hose, for example, were overwhelming. Sometimes, she went into her closet, sat on the floor, and cried. A turning point for Osmond was learning that her mother, who had nine children, experienced depression after she gave birth to her last child. "It's really okay to fall apart because, you know, you're not alone," her mother told her. Society expects mothers to be happy, Osmond pointed out, but there are other realities—days of exhaustion and disappointment—that need to be discussed openly, and she urged women to help each other through this kind of crisis.

Two years later, in 2001, the topic was headline news. "Millions of new mothers are at risk. One out of three women suffers from some kind of postpartum depression," Oprah

Top: Ayelet Waldman and Oprah discuss Waldman's controversial confession, April 20, 2005.

Bottom: Marie Osmond discusses her postpartum depression, October 25, 1999.

Top: Dr. Deborah Sichel, Mike Anfinson, Heidi Anfinson (on screen), and Oprah talk about the dangers of postpartum psychosis and depression, November 7, 2001.

Middle: Doug Kramp, Erin Kramp, and Oprah discuss Erin's decision to record videos for her one-year-old daughter, Peyton, after being diagnosed with cancer, April 20, 1998.

Bottom: Erin Kramp, April 20, 1998.

informed her viewers. She told the story of Melanie Stokes, a young woman who committed suicide not long after giving birth to a baby girl. Stokes complained to her doctors that she felt as if her brain were disintegrating, but they didn't know what to do with her. Her parents said she would be alive today if someone had diagnosed postpartum depression, which is a treatable condition. There are women who are particularly vulnerable to the effects of hormonal shifts after delivery, and Stokes was one of them. So were Andrea Yates, who drowned her five children in the bathtub, and Heidi Anfinson, who killed her two-week-old son.

In 2005, actress Brooke Shields told Oprah her story of acute postpartum depression, a feeling so intense that she feared she would never bond with her baby. She was able to get medical help and urged other women to do the same. "Don't ignore the symptoms of postpartum depression out of embarrassment or shame," she said. "Find out what medicine is available. You don't have to be miserable." Oprah hoped that hearing these stories would help women who were confused by their emotions after pregnancy and delivery "to see a little piece of light in their own lives," and realize that they were not alone.

Mothers have a way of rising above adversity, and *The Oprah Winfrey Show* often paid tribute to extraordinary women who were an inspiration to their children. There were the brave mothers of 9/11. Genelle Guzman and her friend Rosa tried to escape from the burning towers together. The whole time, Rosa's only thoughts were for her daughter. She perished, but Guzman survived and appeared on *Oprah* to tell Rosa's child about her mother's bravery and devotion.

Erin Kramp made an indelible impression on everyone who saw her on *The Oprah Winfrey Show*. She was happily married to her husband, Doug, and the mother of a one-year-old daughter, Peyton, when she learned that she had cancer. She accepted the fact that her time with her family was limited and started recording loving video messages for her daughter. Kramp tried to pull together a lifetime of advice for the child who would have to grow up without her, including what she called "girl talk": "Try to pick out makeup that makes it look natural, like you're not wearing any makeup; never get your hair cut if you're going through a difficult, emotional time; don't buy faddish clothes; be a good listener; and when it comes to a husband, pick a very nice guy who has a lot of backbone." Kramp distinguished her death with grace and purpose, and left a unique legacy for her daughter, who would treasure her companionship and advice for the rest of her life.

Women who went to work were afforded the same careful attention by *The Oprah Winfrey Show* as women with more traditional roles. Shows such as "Working with a Sexist" encouraged women to speak up for themselves in the workplace. Oprah also inspired women to be entrepreneurial. Many of the products she presented as her "Favorite Things"—Spanx shapewear, for example— were created by women, for women. One viewer observed that "any kind of big, successful woman has gained knowledge and insights from Oprah . . . 'Here's the owner of Spanx, here's how she came up with the idea, here are the tools you need.' . . . It's almost like a learning hour, a self-help hour." And at the center of that hour was the best example—Oprah herself. She started her own company, founded her own magazine, launched her own network, became a billionaire, and, somehow, remained the down-to-earth girlfriend who still counted her blessings.

Oprah encouraged women to identify a passion, or a talent, and find a way to use it with purpose, as she had done in her own life. She often told the story of her early days in television. When she started out as a reporter, she was criticized for having too much empathy for her subjects: Journalists were supposed to be impartial and her emotions were getting in the way. But when she hosted her own talk show, her empathy—her ability to forge immediate bonds with her guests—was key to her success. It was all about finding the right place for the right talents.

In thinking about women, Oprah looked around the globe and into the future. How could *The Oprah Winfrey Show* have an impact on subsequent generations of women? Young women everywhere felt connected to Oprah. They sat with their mothers, sisters, and friends—and sometimes alone, appreciating

Top: Spanx creator Sara Blakely and Oprah, February 1, 2007.

Bottom: Suze Orman and Oprah, February 13, 2008.

The Oprah Winfrey Show began broadcasting with subtitles in Saudi Arabia in November 2004.

her comforting maternal presence in an empty home—watching the show and absorbing its lessons. On the episode "Empowering Girls," for example, Oprah taught them that "strength, self-esteem, and independence" were all within reach: Speaking out is empowerment, she said.

Learning how to manage money was empowering, too. Many women, even successful ones, had no idea how to spend or save responsibly. They could take a step in the right direction by downloading a free electronic version of Suze Orman's best-selling book, *Women & Money*, which was made available to them through *The Oprah Winfrey Show*. "This great offer came right from Suze's heart, because she is passionate about women gaining control over their finances," said Oprah. Orman wanted women "to save their money and save themselves," and they eagerly sought her advice. During the thirty-three-hour window when the ebook was available, there were 1.1 million downloads of the English edition and 19,000 downloads of the Spanish edition.

The Oprah Winfrey Show spoke to women everywhere, including in the Arab world. According to the *New York Times*, it became "the highest-rated English language program among women 25 and younger, an age group that makes up about a third of Saudi Arabia's population." Women who had to cover their faces in public, defer to men, and suppress their intellects and their interests, found a friend and a mentor in Oprah. "Conversations among young women start with, 'Did you see Oprah last night?'" reported a Saudi journalist. "Saudi women say they are drawn to Ms. Winfrey not only because she openly addresses subjects considered taboo locally, but also because she speaks of self-empowerment and change," observed the *Times*. "I feel that Oprah truly understands me," confided an Arab woman named Nayla.

"American women love Oprah Winfrey and Oprah loves them back," noted *U.S. News & World Report*. Oprah understood the wants and needs of her audience because, in the most fundamental ways, she was one of them. "I think I am the viewer," she said. She acknowledged that she experienced the same successes, failures, doubts, hopes, and dreams as any woman. Oprah triumphed over a difficult past, including sexual molestation; an early, unwanted pregnancy; a series of destructive relationships; and drug abuse. She suffered bouts of "man trouble," and struggled with her weight. That's what made her human. But what made her a role model was her ability to pull herself together, stand tall, move ahead, and step purposefully, and always with intent, over whatever minefields life placed in her path.

Maria Shriver

The Power of the Girlfriend

Every woman knows the power of the girlfriend. Girlfriends are there to support you in tough times and celebrate with you in great times. But true girlfriends can be very hard to find. I didn't know it at the time, but in 1978 I was lucky enough to work in Baltimore, Maryland, at WJZ-TV. It turned out to be an incredible job, and I made one of the greatest friends of my life. I was a producer on *PM Magazine*, and Oprah, who was cohosting the show *People Are Talking*, was in the office next to me. Like characters in a sitcom, we lived in the same apartment complex (she was one floor above me and had real furniture). We ate dinner together at the local supermarket, which had a small dining area for people who, like us, had nowhere else to go. And we chatted about guys, television, our weight, our ambitions, life, love, and struggles—you name it, we talked about it.

We came from very different worlds, but we ended up in the same place and had the same interests. We bonded. While Oprah always shared everything about herself and her life, my family was more closed off and private. I can recall beginning many of our conversations by exclaiming, "Oh my god, don't talk about *that*." She was uninhibited and that was exciting to me. She knew, intuitively, how to draw deep and truthful things out of me. Back then, she was a lot like she is today. She had a unique voice, and she was determined to use it to inspire, influence, and impact others, especially women and girls. She often spoke in churches, standing up fearlessly and sharing her journey with congregations. Even then, I was amazed by her audacity and awed by the power of her voice. Although she had a smaller pulpit, so to speak, she was just doing on a local level what she does today on a global scale.

We've always been there for each other through those life-changing moments that can define your life. She came to Los Angeles and stayed with me when she was auditioning for *The Color Purple*. I flew to Chicago to be with her for the taping of her last three shows. She was with me at my wedding and at my parents' funerals. And after my mother and my uncle died in rapid succession, she hosted a "love-fest," an intimate gathering of people on "my team" who would support me when I needed them the most. And what she has done for me on a personal level, she has done for women everywhere. Like a great girlfriend, Oprah "showed up" every day for millions of women. She helped them find untapped reservoirs of strength during difficult times in their lives. On her show, she made a place for women to talk about and listen to the issues that matter, from the practical to the profound. These conversations were respectful and came from a place of compassion. Oprah's show gave her audience an outlet for the fears, doubts, and hopes that many of us keep locked up inside ourselves. She used her platform to grow a television audience into a supportive, thoughtful, and active community of people who set out to be angels (another name for a girlfriend) in one another's lives. This community proved to women that they were not alone with their problems. I believe that was revolutionary.

When I was First Lady of California, I created the Minerva Awards because I wanted to honor women who were serving on the front lines of humanity with courage, compassion, wisdom, and strength. Our Minerva Award recipients were remarkable women, well-known and not well-known, who stepped out of their own comfort zones, saw where they themselves could (where they must) make a difference, and went out and did it. The name Minerva came from the Roman goddess portrayed on the California state seal. As the goddess of wisdom, she's a peacemaker; but when it's time to fight for something, she puts on her helmet and becomes a warrior. I think Oprah embodies those same qualities and characteristics. She truly is a wise warrior, and I was honored to present her with a Minerva Award in 2010.

I am also honored to have her as my friend. I suspect millions of her viewers feel the same way. She is patient and compassionate, and she has a terrific sense of humor. I always say that I don't need to go to a therapist because when Oprah's on the phone, she talks me through it. That has been her gift to all women—talking us through it, whatever it may be. I am incredibly proud of the success she has attained. It never surprised me because she always had a voice that was bigger than she was, and she always wanted to use it for something larger than herself. She has changed the lives of millions and millions of people. There is no question that women around the world are more understanding, more informed, and certainly more empowered thanks to the daily classroom that was *The Oprah Winfrey Show* and the force of her personality, intelligence, and character.

Oprah is one of my oldest and dearest friends in the world. I love her deeply, and I believe that she is truly one of the most extraordinary Architects of Change on the planet.

And she is, and will always be, a girlfriend to the world.

Oprah & Gayle's Adventures

In the tradition of Lucy and Ethel, Laverne and Shirley, Ralph Kramden and Ed Norton, Fred and Barney, and other legendary television teams, Oprah and Gayle have delighted viewers with their madcap adventures. Best friends for more than thirty-five years, they have moved through life sharing all the significant moments—large and small, serious and funny—that are the hallmark of the greatest friendships. Their on-air road trips were comedic masterpieces because they enabled viewers to see them in all their spontaneous glory. When they drove cross-country in a Chevrolet, Oprah pumped gas for the first time in twenty-three years and complained about the cost. They got lost in Las Vegas, crashed a wedding, and engaged in a get-out-of-the-car argument about the meaning of the Paul Simon song "Graceland," a blowup that Oprah thought might end the trip and their friendship. On an excursion to Texas, Gayle consumed legendary quantities of food at an old-fashioned state fair and, during a spa vacation, tried, but failed, to overcome her fear of heights by dangling from a high wire in a trust exercise called a "Swing and a Prayer." They camped at Yosemite National Park, visited an Amish community, and faced the ultimate challenge when they "traveled back in time" to the year 1628 and tried living without electricity, indoor plumbing, or, much to their shock, underwear.

Even as viewers laughed at the antics they witnessed during Gayle's record 141 appearances on *The Oprah Winfrey Show*, they appreciated the deep and enduring bond the women shared, a bond that transcended time and place, survived squabbles, and reminded everyone that there is nothing quite so wonderful as a best friend.

Oprah, Ali Wentworth, and Gayle King at the Texas State Fair in Dallas, October 26, 2009.

Clockwise from top: Oprah and Gayle riding mules, Yosemite National Park, November 3, 2010; Gayle and Oprah embark on a five-part road trip, September 18, 2006. Oprah and Gayle under a tunnel tree, Yosemite National Park, October 29, 2010.

Oprah & Gayle's Adventures

Gayle and Oprah visit Miraval Spa in Tucson, Arizona, May 14, 2007.

Clockwise from top left:
Gayle and Oprah spend
two days at PBS's *Colonial
House* to see how people
lived four hundred years
ago; Oprah and Gayle pick
vegetables; Oprah and
Gayle share dinner with
their colonial neighbors,
May 17, 2004.

Star Power

"The essence of style is how you live your life; what you do with your life."

– Oscar de la Renta

In addition to convincing viewers to embrace the unfamiliar, *The Oprah Winfrey Show* set new standards for the "cultural" content presented on talk shows—especially celebrity culture.

"I pretty much just do whatever Oprah tells me to," says Liz Lemon, Tina Fey's character on the hit comedy series *30 Rock*. The fictional Lemon, along with millions of *real* viewers, considered *The Oprah Winfrey Show* to be their most trusted arbiter of culture and style. The show's unassailable tastemaker, Oprah Winfrey herself, could be counted on to proffer smart, sensible, and personal advice about everything from philosophy to panty hose. She was Head Curator at the Museum of Life, the person whose imprimatur, or seal of approval, guaranteed quality and ignited rapid (and usually rampant) popularity and profits, a much-studied phenomenon dubbed the "Oprah Effect."

She had the power to bestow success on anyone and anything she endorsed, but with that power came tremendous responsibility. What Oprah's audience knew for sure was that she was motivated by the purest intention. "I always take the elevator downstairs by myself before every show, and regardless of whether the show is Priscilla Presley or mom makeovers, my prayer, my meditation, my thought for myself is 'How can I best be used . . . to transform the way people see themselves, to uplift, to enlighten, to encourage, to entertain?'" In the words of Maya Angelou, "When you know better, you do better." Oprah wanted to turn her viewers into discerning consumers, and she was as dedicated to promoting their cultural well-being as she was to improving their physical, emotional, and spiritual health.

For many people, the word *culture* is synonymous with a raised pinkie and stifled yawns. *The Oprah Winfrey Show* addressed this very prejudice in a 1995 show titled "How to Get Yourself Some Culture." People get stuck in a rut, Oprah suggested to her audience. They watch the same television programs, eat the same food, and rarely try anything new because they are afraid to venture beyond their comfort zone. Oprah's guests on that show, the Campsey family, fell into that category—in fact they gave themselves a low "2" on the "cultural-appreciation scale." But Oprah broadened their horizons when she arranged for the Campseys to

Oprah and John Travolta dance while he sings "I've Got a Crush on You," March 25, 2003.

sample Caribbean food and attend a performance of the innovative musical show *Stomp*. They were a little suspicious of the exotic dinner, but they loved going to the theater and vowed to do it more often.

On the same episode, a young couple spent a delightful evening at a poetry slam, and five bachelors who generally hung out in their neighborhood bar agreed to accompany art advisor Greg Hubert to a tony fundraiser at the Chicago Art Institute. The men were shocked to discover that they responded to the art, *and* that the museum was a great place to meet eligible young women. High culture, Oprah pointed out, does not have to be "hoighty-toighty-snooty-pooty." Instead of being intimidated by what you *don't* know, cultivate a personal aesthetic, she advised. What do *you* think is beautiful? If you had a billion dollars, what works of art would you buy for your home? In addition to visiting museums, try going to the theater, the circus, the opera, movies. *Read*. The point of the show was that "culture," however alien, could—and should—be approached with

an open mind. When Oprah encouraged her audience to enter worlds they avoided because they felt ignorant or insecure, they became confident and curious. With her guidance, they read books they might have dismissed as being too intellectual, and developed an appetite for "exotica" such as poetry and documentary films. With each experience, they *grew*.

In addition to convincing viewers to embrace the unfamiliar, *The Oprah Winfrey Show* set new standards for the "cultural" content presented on talk shows—especially celebrity culture. Stars usually appeared on talk shows to promote new projects. But when Oprah welcomed luminaries onto *her* stage, self-promotion was not an acceptable raison d'être: "You can't just throw celebrities on the show unless they can add something to the idea or can further the mission in some way," she insisted. They had to have something to say, *and* they had to say it in a way that resonated with her audience.

The list of celebrities who appeared on *The Oprah Winfrey Show* reflected the brightest

Oprah tries on a flying harness while visiting Celine Dion at Caesar's Palace in Las Vegas, March 24, 2003.

stars in Hollywood and beyond. But Oprah was more interested in the light *inside*. "I don't care about stars," she said. "What really matters is what's behind that façade . . . the quality of life and energy exuded from the person who is called a star." John Travolta, who appeared on *Oprah* nineteen times, was her idea of the best kind of celebrity, "one of those people who loves life and has such deep compassion and feelings for other people that . . . who he is as a person means more to me than the fact he's a star," she asserted.

Like Travolta, the celebrities who had the most to offer—the ones who were willing to lower the wall that generally prevented viewers from making a real connection with them—were the guests whom Oprah welcomed back repeatedly. Singer Celine Dion was the record-holder, with twenty-seven appearances on the show. She performed, shared her thoughts and feelings about motherhood, had a singing reunion with her parents and brother, and, in one hair-raising episode, taught Oprah a flying stunt at her show at Caesar's Palace in Las Vegas.

Will Smith (seventeen appearances) and his wife, Jada Pinkett Smith (nineteen appearances), talked about parenting and their ongoing love affair in one interview, and on another show, Will threw himself into Oprah's lap. A radiant and visibly pregnant Julia Roberts (twenty-two appearances) revealed to her friend Oprah that she was expecting twins. Halle Berry (twenty-one appearances) celebrated her historic Best Actress Oscar. Beyoncé (nineteen appearances) commiserated with Oprah about the public's untoward interest in the men in their lives (Stedman for Oprah and Jay-Z for Beyoncé) and taught Oprah her sexy "booty shake."

Guests felt so comfortable in Oprah's presence that anything could happen. Funnymen Jim Carrey (fifteen appearances), Tom Hanks (fourteen appearances), Robin Williams (fourteen appearances), and Jerry Seinfeld (fourteen appearances) never failed to charm Oprah with their antics. And Tom Cruise (fourteen appearances) could always be counted on for an energetic interview. But it was the legendary Sir Paul McCartney who was her teenage dream. Oprah looked blissful when they danced together to the

Clockwise from top left: Halle Berry, February 1, 2002; Will Smith and Oprah, February 7, 2005; Beyoncé Knowles and Oprah, September 19, 2003; Oprah embraces Julia Roberts, seven-months pregnant with twins, November 4, 2004.

John Travolta

A Toast to Oprah
Delivered on the occasion of her fiftieth birthday, January 29, 2004

So, in honor of your birthday, I want to make a toast. Now I'm nervous, so bear with me. Now, we need champagne to make a toast. So Cristal Rose—your favorite is Cristal Rose, right? Okay. Well, they, your friends over there, sent over some champagne. So here we go. There we go. So here's a toast. To the most wonderful person in the world—Oprah Winfrey, our friend. And it's not just because you went out of your way to make sure that fifty thousand underprivileged children in South Africa had their first Christmas gift, or that you want to put schools throughout that country, but also because you inject the spirit into our society of life. You care. Your intelligence, your inspiration . . . and you do it all without judging, and because you treat everyone equally important, and this makes you a great American hero. You represent the best of our country and what's possible in our country. But more importantly, you are a citizen of the world, and you are a hero to mankind. So we are better for knowing you, Oprah. We are. And to boot, you are beautiful. You are sexy. You're talented. And we love you so much, we can't take it. To Oprah!

Jett Clipper Ella

In all her years of high-wattage interviews, Oprah placed two people at the top of her list, and for two very different reasons.

Priscilla Presley, Lisa Marie Presley, and Oprah Winfrey, March 29, 2005.

Opposite, top: Oprah visits Tom Cruise in Telluride, Colorado, May 2, 2008.

Opposite, bottom: Oprah and Jay-Z on the stoop of his grandmother's home in Bedford-Stuyvesant, September 24, 2009.

strains of "Yesterday" as the interview ended. Jane Fonda shared insights about aging and demonstrated exercises that proved youth was still on her side. Jay-Z took Oprah to the housing project where he grew up in the Bedford-Stuyvesant section of Brooklyn and to his grandmother's house, where they sat on a stoop and talked about his past.

In all her years of high-wattage interviews, Oprah placed two people at the top of her list, and for two very different reasons. "I will have to say that interviewing Lisa Marie Presley ["An *Oprah* Exclusive: Priscilla and Lisa Marie Presley's First Mother/Daughter Interview Together"] was one of the most interesting I have ever had. I sat down with her thinking, 'Who's there inside the picture, the façade of Lisa Marie Presley?'" Although Presley, the daughter of one American icon and the ex-wife of another, was guarded in the beginning, there was a moment when she dropped her defenses and connected with Oprah. She talked about Elvis, her famous father; her mother; and the hurtful side of fame. "Oprah, Miss Oprah, this seat is hot," Lisa Marie joked, but she offered honest, carefully considered answers to Oprah's most penetrating questions. When discussing Lisa Marie's failed marriage to Michael Jackson, Oprah asked, "Do you think he loved you?" "I don't know the answer to that to be honest with you . . . as much as he was capable of loving somebody," was her guest's candid reply. The interview was full of revelations. "It was just like two people sitting here in my living room," Oprah later recalled.

Most guests felt that way. Oprah had a unique ability to project empathy and to forge an immediate bond with her subject. However, the legendary Elizabeth Taylor was immune to Oprah's charms when she appeared on the show in 1988. Right before the interview, Taylor told Oprah not to ask her anything about her relationships. "That's kind of hard to do when you're Elizabeth Taylor and you've been married seven times," Oprah thought to herself. That meant there was nothing to discuss and, worse, absolutely no chemistry or energy on the stage that day. "It's still painful to watch," Oprah said several years later. Taylor apologized and subsequently made a friendlier appearance on the show, but their failed interview—the one that got away—was the one Oprah would never forget.

The Oprah Winfrey Show launched many stars in its time, notably singer Alicia Keys, who was named a "rising star" on the show during her television debut in 2001, and operatic pop vocal group Il Divo, four talented men handpicked from around the globe by Simon Cowell. Oprah traded stories—and flamboyant fashion accessories—with Lady Gaga and reminisced on set with the cast of *Friends*, as Jennifer Aniston, Courteney Cox, Lisa Kudrow, Matthew LeBlanc, Matthew Perry, and David Schwimmer steeled themselves for the emotionally charged end of their long-running series.

The Oprah Winfrey Show hosted a number of celebrity reunions on its stage, including the memorable assemblage of more than one hundred members of the incredibly entertaining Osmond family, who gathered to sing, dance, and pay tribute to their beloved patriarch, George Osmond, shortly after his death.

One very special reunion was billed as "A dream come true for Oprah." The cast of *The Mary Tyler Moore Show*—Mary herself, Cloris Leachman, Valerie Harper, Ed Asner, Georgia Engel, Gavin MacLeod, and Betty White—joined Oprah on a set that was a re-creation of Mary Richards's apartment and the television station where she worked. The acclaimed series was seminal for Oprah, she revealed, because Mary—a young, single, career woman—was her chief role model when she was growing up.

Clockwise from top left: Alicia Keys, June 21, 2001; Lady Gaga and Oprah, January 15, 2010; Il Divo with Simon Cowell (right), April 4, 2005.

Oprah's celebrity interviews—unscripted, conversational, intimate, honest, and often historic—offered a rare look at the person behind the persona, making it impossible for experienced viewers to accept canned promotional puff pieces in their stead. When they knew better, they expected better.

The Oprah Winfrey Show also approached matters of style and beauty with intention. On *Oprah,* a makeover wasn't just a make-over, it was the external manifestation of a "best life," a chance to be reinvented, or even reborn. A real makeover is more than cosmetic. "I always like it when you can see in the person's eye, something happened," Oprah explained. "So the hairdo, the eyelashes, the clothes, all of that is really secondary to, Did you see yourself differently? Did you see the possibility of what you can be every day in your life?" The busy mom who never took time for herself, the policewoman who had to hide her femininity on the beat, the hearse driver who was required to look somber on the job—these women had forgotten who they were inside. With the help of Oprah's experts, they learned how to dress to express their true, individual beauty.

The Oprah Winfrey Show gave its viewers access to the best style gurus in the business, from supermodels and fashion designers to hair and makeup artists. During one memorable appearance, model and actress Lauren Hutton, more stunning than ever at age fifty, advised viewers to know and accept themselves and extolled the virtues of being an older woman. "I think you learn how to operate the vehicle," she quipped, advocating wearing easy, well-made, affordable clothing and accessories.

Oprah welcomed fashion icon Vera Wang to the show on several occasions, crediting her with creating the gown—the figure-enhancing dazzler that Oprah wore to the 2005 Academy Awards—responsible for giving her "the prettiest day of my life." Wang gave other women *their* prettiest days, too, especially brides. On a show aptly titled "Ultimate Wildest Dreams," several deserving brides who dreamed of wearing Vera Wang but couldn't afford to, were given wedding dresses. Lashia, whose fiancé was serving in

Top: *Friends* cast members Matthew LeBlanc, Lisa Kudrow, David Schwimmer, Courteney Cox, Matthew Perry, Jennifer Aniston, and Oprah, November 20, 2003.

Bottom: Vera Wang and Oprah, September 17, 2010.

Diane von Furstenberg

The Lasting Makeover

Oprah is bigger than life! Her presence is warm, intelligent, and compassionate, but her desire to improve the world and not let it slide into mediocrity is what I admire most about her.

At a time when television continues to sink to the lowest common denominator, Oprah fights to raise its level.

She is honest and demands honesty. She is loving and distributes love. She is beautiful and beautifies her audience. She allows people to dream and goes beyond their dreams.

In her makeover shows, women get transformed. But not just on the outside: Their confidence comes out and stays with them.

When you think of Oprah, you don't immediately think about fashion, and yet she has done so much to show women how to feel good about themselves and improve who they are!

That will last, and that is what matters.

Afghanistan, said that finding the perfect man was a cinch compared to finding the perfect dress. She fantasized about having a Vera Wang gown, and Oprah made that fantasy come true.

When Oprah heard that eight out of ten women in America were wearing the wrong size bra (and the wrong jeans), she decided to launch "A Bra and Jean Intervention." Her producers set up a frilly pink bra boutique on set—complete with eight thousand bras—and welcomed thirty-five fitters from Nordstrom to banish sag from the audience once and for all. By the end of the session, every woman was happily ensconced in the right bra, standing tall and looking *very* pretty. Jeans were difficult to fit, too, top stylist Stacy London warned. A woman should try on at least twenty pairs before deciding on one. After the "Intervention" aired, suddenly *everyone* was an expert on how to defy gravity.

Top: Studio Two is transformed into a bra-fitting store in order to help audience members find the right bra, November 15, 2005.

Bottom: Mara Schiavocampo, digital correspondent for *NBC Nightly News with Brian Williams*, traveled to Japan and India to discover what these women considered beautiful, November 20, 2008.

Ralph Lauren gives Oprah a tour of his family's Rocky Mountain retreat, May 18, 2011.

Supermodels Christie Brinkley, Stephanie Seymour, Beverly Johnson, and Cheryl Tiegs made a spectacular quartet on the show "Supermodel Legends." Their fabulous faces and figures belied their over-forty, over-fifty, and even over-sixty, ages. But the wisdom they shared about growing older, self-image, and inner beauty was more inspirational than any how-to tips. Beauty was, after all, highly subjective. *The Oprah Winfrey Show* invited viewers to take a more global approach to the subject by exploring "Beauty Secrets from Around the World." They learned that some Japanese women maintain their pearly complexions with a "bird poop" facial made from nightingale droppings. In Iran, nose jobs are considered status symbols, prompting certain women who have not had surgery to wear bandages. And in Mauritania, fat is considered beautiful. "You can't have a butt too big in Mauritania," Oprah marveled. The underlying point of every show that dealt with fashion or beauty was to make women—and men, on occasion—feel comfortable in their own skin: True beauty begins *inside*.

Oprah extended that philosophy to the home. "It's the place that should rise up to meet you when you enter, and leave you feeling full and filled when you leave," Oprah maintained. Her homes reflected her *interior*, and she hoped to help others make that important connection between self and surroundings. She brought her cameras inside her Chicago residence to illustrate the point, and sometimes she visited the homes of celebrities to show how they expressed themselves in their personal spaces.

"It's been a dream of mine to sit down on camera with American icon Ralph Lauren and see how he lives," Oprah told her viewers in 2011. For the first and only time ever, Ralph Lauren allowed Oprah and her cameras inside the cabins that make up his family compound on the magnificent seventeen-thousand-acre Double RL Ranch just outside Telluride, Colorado. The visit provided a rare view of the man, his family, and the private world they share in their mountain retreat. During the interview, Oprah established that there was perfect synergy between Lauren's

Before (top) and after (bottom) images of Nate Berkus's transformation of a 319-square-foot studio, September 24, 2002.

creative vision and his environment. "I'm not about fashion," he said. "I'm about living, and that's been my whole career. And the clothes that I've designed and everything I've done is about life and how people live and how they want to live and how they dreamed they'd live, and that's what I do." Lauren's splendid and beautifully appointed ranch was a memorable sight, but his understanding of the importance of place was truly impressive.

Oprah added design expert Nate Berkus to her dream team of "Best Life" advisors to educate viewers about the significance and potential beauty of *their* homes. His first project for *The Oprah Winfrey Show* was a Herculean task: Berkus was asked to turn a drab, 319-square-foot studio apartment into a functional *and* attractive home for a young career woman in Boston. When he finished, the on-air "reveal" made Oprah—and the studio audience—gasp. "That's the best damn job I ever saw," she announced. In Berkus's hands, the tiny room had become a miniature palace that served a myriad of purposes: a bedroom, dining room, office, and living room rolled into one exquisite and beautifully decorated space.

For the next eight years, Berkus worked with design-challenged families and individuals to improve their surroundings. The Hale-Jo family was a case in point. Kari and Dave lived with their two-year-old son, Ty, in a little house. Their lives changed dramatically when they offered to share their home with their three young nieces, whose father was unable to care for them. Suddenly, their small space was a big problem. Oprah dispatched Nate Berkus to the rescue, and the happy Hale-Jos became the recipients of an expanded home with room for everyone. Miraculously, Berkus and his team accomplished the expansion and renovation in fifteen days.

Sometimes celebrities needed as much help as ordinary people. Actor Jerry O'Connell invited Berkus to turn his superannuated "man cave," complete with bobbleheads, old electronics, and ill-appointed rooms, into a proper, grown-up home. Berkus also tackled

Before (top) and after (bottom) images of Kirstie Alley's kitchen makeover, November 12, 2004.

the job of designing and building a new kitchen for actress Kirstie Alley, who wept when she saw the completed room, a Mediterranean retreat that could truly be the heart of her home. When Nate Berkus transformed spaces, he transformed lives.

Oprah's "you deserve the best" approach to entertainment and domestic life also applied to products. The same way that she shared her favorite reads with her Book Club, she shared her favorite things with her favorite people: her viewers. When Oprah found something she loved, whether it was a Kindle or a cake, she featured it on the show, and presto!—that item generally experienced stratospheric growth. Some called it the "Oprah Effect," others the "O Factor." But whatever the name, the consensus was that "there's no advertising power greater than the power of the O." But the word "advertising" was a misnomer, because Oprah's endorsement could never be bought. She was motivated by passion, and passion alone.

Whenever Oprah mentioned a product, it was not uncommon for phone lines to blow up, websites to crash, and inventories to sell out. Carol's Daughter, a homegrown company specializing in artisanal beauty products, was enjoying two million dollars in sales when the line was featured on *The Oprah Winfrey Show*, and that happy two million turned into an ecstatic *thirty* million. Oprah praised a silver ox-cuff watch sold by the women's store Chico's, and before the show was over, customers had purchased all five thousand of the watches in stock, and within a few days, had ordered forty thousand more. Interestingly, although the watch was available in gold and brass, most customers wanted the exact one Oprah had. Owning the same products Oprah used made viewers feel close to her.

Oprah Winfrey was a cultural ambassador who raised her audience's consciousness and expectations. She invited them to aim higher, to demand the best, and to learn, as she had learned, that experiencing enrichment, transformation, and fulfillment in their own lives would inspire them to share those feelings with others.

Music to Our Ears

"I gotta feelin' that today's gonna be a good day," sang the Black Eyed Peas as Oprah moved to the beat on an outdoor stage overlooking Chicago's Michigan Avenue. It was the kickoff party for the twenty-fourth season of *The Oprah Winfrey Show*, and as Oprah quickly realized, it rocked! Her producers surprised her with an audience of twenty-one thousand people who performed a choreographed flash-mob dance to an "Oprah-cized" version of the group's hit song. Oprah loved it. "That was the coolest thing ever," she said. In fact, some of her favorite moments on *Oprah* were spent with stars from the music world. She sat at the piano with Sir Paul McCartney, saw her wildest dreams come true when she danced with Tina Turner and, on another occasion, sang with her childhood idol, Diana Ross. She reveled in the music of Bono, Stevie Nicks, the Judds, actor/crooner Jamie Foxx, and other favorites. For Oprah, any day that included legendary musicians and their music was "a good day."

Clockwise from top: Bono performs in Australia with Oprah and ultimate viewers in the audience, January 20, 2011; Oprah and Diana Ross, April 5, 2000; Oprah and Tina Turner, February 21, 1997.

Clockwise from top left: Jamie Foxx and Oprah, November 29, 2005; Oprah with the audience during the "Rock Goddesses of the '70s and '80s" show, April 13, 2011; Sheryl Crow and Stevie Nicks, April 13, 2011; The Black Eyed Peas perform "I Gotta Feeling" while a flash-mob surprises Oprah with a choreographed dance on Michigan Avenue in Chicago, September 10, 2009; Naomi and Wynonna Judd, September 14, 2010.

Julia Roberts

Close to Perfect
Delivered at the 33rd Annual Kennedy Center Honors

It is a universal conversation starter: Did you see what was on *Oprah* today?

It creates calm at the dentist; it can make a friend of a stranger on a bus; it binds mothers and daughters of all generations.

Oprah Gail Winfrey.

To be asked to speak on an occasion such as this has, to be honest, kept me up at night—all night—many, many nights.

It is not what to say, but could there ever be enough time to say it?

And I've been told I have three minutes.

So let's break it down here in front of God and the president. I think she is pretty damn close to perfect. And I don't mean boring, run-of-the-mill perfect. I mean fabulous, shining, margarita-drinking perfect. But as a friend, I must reveal and yet not tell too much.

In my late-night ponderings, I realize it is not the place she holds in the world, but how she holds it. And how, after so many years, the world holds her back.

The Oprah Winfrey Show first aired in 1986. I was just out of high school and had no idea that in three years I would be invited for the first time to appear on that show.

I was terrified, and Oprah was kind and supportive.

It is now one of the delights of my life that she is my friend.

The Kennedy Center Honor is—as I understand it—a lifetime achievement award for entertainment and advancement of American culture.

Well, she has done that and then some! She is tireless, brilliant, hilarious, and compassionate. She comes on television every day of the week and is our friend, a teacher, a leader, a listener.

The first time I heard about a better-fitting bra, the inner workings of Chicago's sewage system, "Favorite Things," or a fascinating politician named Barack Obama was on the *Oprah* show.

She has led and taught and guided us all in such a gentle and consistent way that I think we have all not only benefited, we have, whether for a moment or a lifetime, become the best that we could be.

I would usually never be so bold as to speak for a culture of women, but I feel great confidence saying on behalf of the women of America: We thank you, and we are in debt to you.

Now, in the spirit of *The Oprah Winfrey Show,* if everyone could reach under their seats . . .

I'm so proud of you. I love you. Congratulations.

"You Get a . . ."

When Oprah announced her Favorite Things, they became everyone's favorite things. An eclectic mix of "bests," from croissants to cars, Oprah's 283 picks shot to the top of holiday shopping lists and delighted lucky recipients.

Oprah, November 22, 2004.

$100 Kiva Gift Card, Courtesy of Groupon
$250 Gift Card to Target
"The Four Agreements"
2 VIP Tickets to the Beyoncé Experience with Robin Thicke
A Course in Weight Loss by Marianne Williamson
A New Earth by Eckhart Tolle (book and audio tape)
Adidas Mei Mind and Body Footwear
Alexander Wood Holiday Greeting Cards
America 24/7
Andre Walker Hair Care Products
Apple Bottom Jeans by Nelly
Apple iPad
Apple iPod*
Apple iPod Nano
B'Day Deluxe Edition by Beyoncé
Baker's Edge Brownie Pan
Baker's Edge Simple Lasagna Pan
Balboa Medallion Rolling Duffel by Toss Designs
Banana Republic Cashmere Sweaters
Barefoot Dreams Robes
BeBe Winans' *My Christmas Prayer* and Starbucks Gift Card
Beecher's "World's Best" Mac 'N' Cheese
Bette by Bette Midler
BlackBerry 7105t from T-Mobile
BlackBerry Wireless E-mail Device
Bliss Labs Glamour Gloves and Glamour Glove Gel
Bourjois Lip Products
Breville Panini Press from Williams-Sonoma*
Brownies from Moveable Feast Geneva
Burberry Coat
Burberry Purse
Burberry Quilted Jacket and Cashmere Scarf
C and C California T-shirts
Cambio Jeans
Centerville Pie Company's Chicken Pie
Cezanne McClennan Memory Trunk
Chanel Ombre Essentielle Soft Touch Eyeshadow in Nomade and Tigre
Chantecaille Protected Paradise Compacts
Ciao Bella Blood Orange Sorbetto
Citrus Tote
Clarins Sun Care
Clarisonic Skin Care System
Claus Porto Soaps from Lafco New York
Clé de Peau Extra Silky Lipstick
Cliff and Buster Macaroons
Clinique Quick Eyes Cream Shadows in Starlit Pink, Truffle, Sparkling Nude, Cocoa Shimmer, and Sunlit Palm
Cocoon Fine Silk Scarves
Couch Sack by Nordic Gear
Courtyard by Marriot Gift Card
CoverGirl LashBlast
Cranberry Creations by Nantucket Clipper
Cuisine Perel Late Harvest Riesling Vinegar
Daryl Sandals by Coach
Davies Gate Allspice Cinnamon Powder Sugar Soak
Decleor Vitaroma Body Sumptuous Anti-Aging Body Cream
Decoded by Jay-Z
Dell 30" Wide-Screen LCD TV
Dell Pocket DJ
DonorsChoose.org Gift Card, Courtesy of Bing.com
Dooney & Bourke Leather Duffle Bag
Dream a Dream by Charlotte Church
DreamTime Foot Cozys
Dreyer's/Edy's Frozen Fruit Bars
Ego Waterproof Sound Case by Atlantic
Eileen Fisher Hooded Waffle-Weave Merino Stretch Zip Cardigan and Merino Stretch Drawstring Pant
Elfa Customizable Closet System from the Container Store
Embroidered Tunic from Boston Proper
Everyday Grace by Marianne Williamson
Faith by Kenny G
Fashion Active Labs Perfect Tee
Fat Witch Baby Gift Tin
Fifi & Romeo custom-made doggie clothes
Five-Year Netflix Membership
Flannel Tory Tote and Flannel Reva Ballerina Flat by Tory Burch
FoodSaver Vac 800 by Tilia, Inc.
Frames by Jay Strongwater
Frederic Fekkai Crème Luxueuse, Apple Cider Clean Shampoo & Conditioner
French Press Coffee Pot from Bodeim Available at Starbucks
Fresh Milk Bath Products and Lotion
Frontgate's Panasonic Portable DVD Player
GAP Body Terrycloth Collection
Garmin International's Garmin Nuvi 250 GPS Device
Garrett Popcorn's CaramelCrisp and CheeseCorn*
Garrett's Special Limited-Edition Favorite Things Tin
Ghirardelli Brownie Mix
Ginger Souffle & Olive Oil Chips
Givenchy Footless Pantyhose
Gladware Products
Godiva Carmel-Nut Bouchees
Good Karmal Mini Crates
Gourmet Florida Key Lime Bundt Cake
Greenberg Smoked Turkeys

Growing Pains by Mary J. Blige
Hallmark (PRODUCT) RED wrapping paper and cards
Hand-blown Crystal Champagne Glasses by Deborah Ehrlich
Havaianas
HDTV Refrigerator with Weather and Info Center from LG Electronics
Herb Savor by Prepara
Hewlett Packard Digital Camera, Printer and Dock
Holiday Favorites Assortment from Talbott Teas
Hot Chocolate Powder by MarieBelle
If You Give a Pig a Pancake by Laura Numeroff
Illuminations by Josh Groban
Illustrated Discovery Journal by Sarah Ban Breathnach
InStyle December Issue
Italian Water Garden Tea Service at Room With A View
J. Lo Velour Sweatsuit
Jessica Leigh Diamond Earrings by Dana Rebecca Designs
Judith Ripka Eclipse Earrings
Judith Ripka Two Necklace
Kai Body Butter and Body Buffer
Kashmere Shawl Collar Robe
Key Lime Pie by Little Pie Company
Kiehl's Limited Edition Gift Box
KN Karen Neuburger Boyfriend Pajamas
KN Karen Neuburger CoolDry Comfort Sleepwear
KN Karen Neuburger Pajamas and lounge socks
KN Karen Neuburger Pink Ribbon Signature Collection
Kyocera Ceramic Cutlery Set by Ming Knives
La Brea Bakery Granola
La Mer Body Serum
Lafco House and Home Collection Candle Set
Lands End Zip Top Tote
Laura Mercier Products
Laurent de Clau Mustard
Lavender Filled Linens
Le Creuset Custom Oprah Cookware
Le Mystère Tisha Bra
Leather Bag by Maria Lyons
Lee Middleton Original Dolls
Let It Be Me by Johnny Mathis
Lippmann Collection Nail Polish in Don't Call Me Baby; Laura Mercier Lip Glace in Bonbon; Jillian Dempsey for Avon Signature Horizon Blush in Coral
Liquid Candles from Lampe-Fleur by Sarut NYC
Lollia Lifestyle Collection Hand Cream and Foaming Bubble Bath
Lovely by Sarah Jessica Parker
Low Fat Cookies from Nancy's Healthy Kitchen
lululemon Relaxed Fit Pants
M.A.C. Cosmetic Carrying Case
Madison Patent Large Sophia Satchel by Coach
Magaschoni Embellished Tunic and Leggings
Mar-a-Lago Mango Chutney
Mar-a-Lago Turkey Burger
Marchon Eyewear
Maybelline New York Mineral Power
Maytag Neptune Top-Load Washer and Drying Center
Melamine Bowls, Measuring Cups and Spoons from Williams-Sonoma
Melted Chocolate Cake Batter
Meryl Jazz Pants by FILA
Miracle by Kenny G
Miraclebody Jeans by Miraclesuit
Miraval Resort and Spa Paid Trip
Miss Rona's Lavender Applesauce
Motorola T-900 Talkabout Messaging Device
Museum Automatic Arte Watch by Movado
My Twinn Doll
NARS Kabuki Artisan Botan Brush
Neiman Marcus Coconut Macaroons
Nicole by OPI Nic's Sticks Paint & Go Nail Lacquer
Nike "Free Run+" Shoes
Nike Air Prestos
Nike Dri-FIT Workout Outfit
Nike Free 5.0 iD
Nikon D3100 Digital SLR Camera
Noël by Josh Groban
Nonnie's Traditional Southern Pound Cake
Nordstrom Lingerie
O, The Oprah Magazine
O, The Oprah Magazine Cookbook from Hyperion Books
O's Guide to Life
Oatmeal Cookie Dough from Fox & Obel Market
Obrycki's Crab Cakes
OfficeMax Gift Certificate
Olay Daily Renewal Body Wash
Old Navy Terry Cover-up
Oprah's Favorite Things Shopping Bag from The Container Store
Origins A Perfect World White Tea Body Cream
Panasonic 4-in-1 Digital Camera from Frontgate
Perfect Endings Cupcakes from Williams-Sonoma
Philip Stein 25th Anniversary "Oprah" Watch
Philip Stein Teslar Diamond Watch
Philip Stein Teslar Watch
Philosophy "Hope in a Jar"**
Philosophy "Grace" basket
Philosophy "Rainbow Connection" Bath Oil
Philosophy "The Gingerbread Man"

Philosophy make-up and shampoo gift bag
Physicians Formula Mineral Wear Talc-Free Mineral Face Powder SPF 16 in Soft Green and Concealer Stick SPF 15 in Light, Soft Green, and Soft Yellow
Picnic Backpack
Pillsbury Home Baked Classics Frozen Biscuits
Piper-Heidsieck Champagne in Baby Piper Bottles
Polaroid Joy Cam
Prescriptives AnyWear Multi-Purpose Makeup Stick SPF 15
Pure Color Cords
Pure Simplicity Pumpkin Purifying Mask
Rachel Pally Swing Turtleneck and Sailor Pants
Ralph Lauren Black Label Cashmere Slim Fit Crewneck Sweater
Ralph Lauren "The Oprah Sweater"
Ralph Lauren Long Sleeve Open Placket Sweater and Cashmere Cable Throw
Reebok's Fusion DMX-10
Ribbon Crusher Hat
Rimmel Mousse Blush
Rituals: Light for the Soul Candle and Bowl
Romanza by Andrea Bocelli
Roomba Floor Vac
Rose Hill Ceramic Dishes
Royal Caribbean Allure of the Seas Cruise
Ruby Slipper Water Globe
Samsung Progressive HD Camcorder SC-HMX10C
Samsung SGH-v205 Mobile Phone and Camera
Sarabeth Jams
Scents and Candles from The GAP/ Elton John Candles by Slatkin
Scrabble App for the iPad by Electronic Arts
Scrabble Premier Edition from Hasbro
Season 25 T-Shirt from the O Store
Shabby Chic T-shirt Sheets
Shaklee Get Clean Starter Kit
Shanghai Tang Silk Pajamas and Slippers
Shu Uemura Mini Eyelash Curler
Silhouette Minimal X Sunglasses
Silver Ox Cuff Watch
Smartees Doll
Soinicare Electric Toothbrush
Sony BRAVIA LX900 HDTV with 3D
Sony DCR-DVD200 Handycam
Sony VAIO FJ Notebook
Sony VAIO S260 Notebook Computer
Sophie Jewelry Box from Pottery Barn
Spa Fleurs Sandals
Spanx Footless Pantyhose
Special Teas Fine Tea Gift Certificate
Sue Shanahan Portrait
Susan Abbott Collage Painting
Talking Photo Album by Sharper Image
Talking Picture Frame from Brookstone
Talking Teddy Telegram
Target Beach Towel
Testimony: Volume 1, Life & Relationship by India.Arie
The Artisan Stand Mixer from KitchenAid Appliances
The Beginning by the Black Eyed Peas
The Book of Awakening by Mark Nepo
The Christmas Album by Johnny Mathis
The Complete George Winston Box Set
The Discovery Channel's *Planet Earth* DVD Set
The Evolution of Robin Thicke by Robin Thicke
The Gemstar REX 1100 eBook from RCA
The Magellan RoadMate 700
The Neiman Marcus Cookbook
The Oprah Winfrey Show 20th Anniversary Collection DVD Collection
The Original Noël Jingle Bell Rock Santa
The Pillars of the Earth by Ken Follett
The Power of Now by Eckhart Tolle
The Screwpull Gift Set by Williams-Sonoma
The Thin Profile CD System by Brookstone
The Wiggly Giggly Ball
Thomas Pink shirts
Together CD and Book
Toywatch Watch
Tube Readers from Micro Vision Optical
UGG Australia Classic Crochet Tall Boot
UGG Australia Sheepskin Boot
UGG Australia's Uptown Boot
UGG Classic Short Boot
UGG Classic Sparkles Boot
United Artists 90th Anniversary Prestige Collection
Volkswagen 2012 Beetle
Wafer-Thin CD System from Brookstone
Warner Brothers Looney Tune Slippers
Weber Genesis EP-310
Weber Q Grill and Cart
Weber Style Tongs, Weber Style Spatula, Weber Grill Brush
Wide-brimmed Canvas Hate from Hat Attack
Williams-Sonoma Croissants**
Williams-Sonoma Home Bedding
Women by Annie Leibovitz
Your Secret Love by Luther Vandross
YSL Eye Shadow Duo in Golden Sand/Brown Earth; Palette Pop Collector Powder for Face & Cheeks; Pop Stick Blush in Vanilla/Chocolate and Strawberry/Raspberry; Rouge Pur Lipstick in Pink Orchid

Note: Asterisks following the name of an item denote the number of years it was selected as a "Favorite Thing." No asterisk indicates one year, one askterisk (*) indicates two years, and two asterisks (**) indicate three years.

"You Get a . . ."

Clockwise from bottom: The audience reacts when they discover they are on the "Ultimate Favorite Things" show, November 19, 2010; Oprah gives away a cruise, November 19, 2010, and a new car, November 22, 2010.

"You Get a . . ."

Clockwise from bottom left: Oprah announces on the "Wildest Dreams with Oprah" show that every audience member will receive a brand-new Pontiac G6; audience reactions; an audience member with her new car, September 13, 2004.

Embracing Equality

"We are all more alike, my friends, than we are unalike."

– Maya Angelou

She was fearless; she was unflappable; and she was committed to using *The Oprah Winfrey Show* to promote understanding, acceptance, and ultimately, equality.

"**In the early years of the show,**" Oprah stated, "I felt it a part of my responsibility as an African American, as a person who lived as a minority in this country, to bring issues of racism and prejudice to the forefront of other people's minds." She acted on that belief five months into her first season, when she ignored the warnings of her producers and traveled to Forsyth County, Georgia, thirty-nine miles north of Atlanta, to plant herself at the center of an explosive racial controversy. Incredibly, although it was 1987, not a single African American had lived in Forsyth County for seventy-five years. The story became national news when black protestors challenged the community's de facto segregation policies and were met by residents who threw rocks and chanted "Nigger, go home." The media condemned Forsyth County as a hotbed of racists. But Oprah was determined to understand the people behind the headlines, and when she arrived on the scene, she was the consummate journalist: cool, purposeful, and nonjudgmental.

Dismissing concerns for her personal safety, she invited a group of residents to engage in an open conversation—a town hall meeting, essentially—to explain why their community was all white and, more importantly, why they felt it was their right to keep it that way. "We've decided to come here and talk with the people of this county ourselves . . . to try and understand the feelings and motivations of the people of all-white Forsyth County. That's what we do every day on this show: explore people's feelings," she reminded her viewers as she introduced the broadcast.

As promised, Oprah ardently defended each person's right to free speech, including an arrogant white supremacist who insisted that Martin Luther King, Jr. was a communist, and an outspoken Southerner named Dennis who announced with great conviction that there was a difference between blacks and "niggers." When Oprah pressed for that distinction, Dennis said—to her face—that "blacks" don't cause any trouble, while "niggers" have no regard for their

Oprah and audience member Dennis discuss racism at a town hall meeting in Forsyth County, Georgia, February 9, 1987.

surroundings and turn nice neighborhoods into rat-infested slums.

Oprah's composure and open-mindedness in the face of blatant bigotry enabled the residents to feel increasingly confident about speaking out, and many revealed that they disapproved of the racists in their community (who actually seemed to be in the minority) and were ready for change. "I just hate to think that someone is going to get hurt before the people get some sense about them and talk about this and get it like it's supposed to be . . . black and white together in Forsyth County. There's no other way," insisted one enlightened woman, prompting her neighbors to applaud in agreement.

As viewers watched that day, they learned several important lessons about Oprah Winfrey: She was fearless; she was unflappable; and she was committed to using *The Oprah Winfrey Show* to promote understanding, acceptance, and ultimately, equality. She wanted to make people think about their prejudices against African Americans, gays, women,

the physically handicapped, the elderly—anyone and everyone whose rights were compromised. By opening their minds, she hoped to open their hearts.

As evidenced by her daring trip to Forsyth County, racism was one of Oprah's primary targets. Sometimes, with shows such as "Black Man Prejudice," "My Parent Is a Racist," "Are You a Racist? With the Cast of *Crash*," "Racism in the Neighborhood," and "I Hate Your Interracial Relationship," she attacked the subject head-on, exploring knee-jerk discrimination against blacks. "I want you to be honest right now," Oprah said during one episode. "Have you ever crossed to the other side of the street because a black man was walking behind you? Or have you ever felt uncomfortable when a black man is in the car next to you, and you lock the doors?" Her straightforward questions resonated with her audience and inspired them to challenge their own irrational biases. Jim Rainey, a self-proclaimed racist who appeared on the show in 1990, admitted to bullying blacks

The Oprah Winfrey Show made it possible for viewers to become more knowledgeable—and more compassionate and open-minded—about racial issues.

and doing everything he could to keep them in their place, until, unexpectedly, he was transformed by the love he developed for his biracial grandson.

Some shows turned thought-provoking discussions into eye-opening revelations. "A Study in Prejudice" profiled a dramatic in-studio experiment conducted by educator Jane Elliott. On that day, guests of *The Oprah Winfrey Show* were separated into two groups according to eye color. Elliott stated that the people with brown eyes were superior, while blue-eyed guests were inferior and were to be treated accordingly (just as black people had been). Immediately, the two groups turned against each other, illustrating how quickly prejudice can ignite, and by the time the show was over, they had experienced discrimination firsthand. Shockingly, the power of suggestion extended beyond the studio. Television viewers called in to support Elliott's "theory," some claiming that their brown-eyed children were smarter than their blue-eyed offspring. At the end of the show, Elliott revealed that she had divided the audience to make the point that people have a better chance of understadning prejudice if they experience it. She repeated the experiment on *Oprah* in 1992, with the same dramatic results. "God created one race, the human race, and human beings created racism," she concluded.

Another bold experiment in racism was recounted by college student Josh Solomon, who appeared on *The Oprah Winfrey Show* to share his story about having been "Black for a Day." Solomon ingested a chemical that turned his skin black, shaved his head, and went out into the world as a young African American. He quickly discovered that people treated him differently when they thought he was black: They were suspicious, rude, disrespectful, and hostile. He was turned away from empty restaurants that claimed to have "no room" when he asked for a table, and was followed by apprehensive store detectives while he shopped. White people automatically receive respect, he learned, while black people are constantly forced to prove they deserve it. Oprah pointed out to her audience, "Over the years, I've done at least a hundred shows on racism. And it's so hard to convey what

Josh Solomon (in studio and on screen) and Oprah, February 17, 1995.

being treated like a suspect every day of your life does to your personal psyche."

The Oprah Winfrey Show used the Forsyth County "town hall" model to debate many important topics relating to race in America. In 1992, Oprah went to Los Angeles to host a two-part show on the Rodney King verdict, listening to people express anger, disillusionment, and frustration over police brutality, racism, and the terrible injustice of the verdict that had provoked the catastrophic riot that destroyed property, claimed lives, and engulfed the city in flames. In 1994, the show traveled to Union, South Carolina, to host a heated, open discussion of the Susan Smith case. Smith, a mother who claimed that a black man kidnapped her two young sons during a carjacking, was later revealed to have killed her children herself. The fact that she was quick to blame an African American for her terrible crime—and that people were even quicker to believe her—exposed a deep and chilling vein of bigotry in the modern-day South.

By persistently airing these discussions in America's living rooms, *The Oprah Winfrey Show* made it possible for viewers to become more knowledgeable—and more compassionate and open-minded—about racial issues. History was an important part of the equation. Oprah found tremendous inspiration in the life of Dr. Martin Luther King, Jr.: "Nothing that has happened in my life since I was sixteen years old would have been possible: I wouldn't have been in radio, I wouldn't have been on television, I wouldn't have been who I am, I wouldn't have become what I've become, I wouldn't live where I live. I just wouldn't have the life that I have without Martin Luther King, Jr.," she said. On Martin Luther King, Jr. Day, she often hosted shows that reiterated his powerful messages about brotherhood, nonviolence, and his famous "dream" of true equality.

On show after show, Oprah honored heroes from the front lines of the civil rights movement, including Rosa Parks, an African American woman who, in 1955, refused to surrender her bus seat to a white passenger in segregated Montgomery, Alabama; Ruby Bridges, the six-year-old girl who was the first African American student to integrate the

New Orleans school system; the famous Little Rock Nine of Arkansas; and the Freedom Riders, social activists who came from all over the country to challenge segregation in the South. "People who've come before me were the bridges that I crossed over on," she often said in speeches, and it was very important to her that their legacies remain a part of living history.

The reunion of the Little Rock Nine of Arkansas, January 15, 1996.

Top: Robin Woods Loucks, Dr. Terrence Roberts, Melba Pattillo Beals, Ernest Green, Thelma Mothershed Wair, Jefferson Thomas, Carlotta Walls LaNier, and Minnijean Brown Trickey.

Middle: Robin Woods Loucks, Dr. Terrence Roberts, and David Sontag.

Bottom: Barbara Henry and Ruby Bridges Hall.

Stanley Crouch

A Magical Mississippi Star

Glory is not possible without access to solitude, because the person recognized for a quality that gives glory to individual action knows how to be alone inside the vast space of the self. That is where all universal elements are to be found. This can be greatly aided by education and research, but they together or alone are not enough. Glory more often than not arrives with insights founded in intuition. If very great glory is discovered in universal terms, the one with the necessary level of intuition should be known as what I call a "genius of feeling." Oprah Winfrey is clearly, and beyond question, a genius of feeling. She may not have been at the very beginning of her career, but she emerged as that kind of person from the moment she began to trust her strongest internal impulses and captivated her enormous international audience with the unforced nature of her emotions toward others, which is very difficult to fake over two decades. This did not always come out well, because she, like everybody else, could be had. When she was, the headlines, the breathless and delicious tongue wagging, and the rabid intensity of the gossip dragging like a tail of tin cans tied to the back fender of our "celebrity culture" increased. Sometimes the din rose to heights tantamount to hysteria. Unlike others who are rich and famous, Winfrey may have been hurt, disappointed, even humiliated by her errors in judgment, but she never backed away from what she started. Her sense of integrity is coupled to her belief in equality. As we know, in a time as mesmerized by all kinds of fraud as ours is, integrity comes at a price many feel is just too expensive. Focusing on the importance of equality is out of the question.

The idea of equality is often misunderstood because too many people feel that it means everyone gets the same thing. It does not. It means that everyone should, in theory, get the same chance to function in the mysterious world of talent without any imposed limitations from the mad ground rules of prejudice. In that respect, Oprah Winfrey is one of the most impressive of those who claim to believe in and be dedicated to the principles underlying democracy. Democracy does not claim to be about perfection in our American sense of it as a political force. It is close to the tragic optimism that animates the blues. This sense of equality actually embraces the messiness fundamental to life itself through which transcendence is brought off by endurance, improvisation, and holding on to goals by outlasting the opposition. The blues means continuing and facing up to the intentional or unintentional misinterpretations, the abuses, the hustles, the opportunism, and whatever else might muck up the way we live in the world through policies designed to better, or improve, the life of human beings.

The sense of equality that Oprah Winfrey obviously believes in is second in its depth to none that I know of in our time—or to any from a previous period. She is the only person from the world of entertainment who has done enough to be seriously mentioned in a list that includes Abigail Adams, Harriet Tubman, Elizabeth Cady Stanton, Susan B. Anthony, and Eleanor Roosevelt. This would seem absurd to say if Oprah Winfrey were not the subject of the statement. This woman has done it all with grace, spit, grit, bucks, and mother wit, turning them all like influential mobiles determined by her will to realize what the saxophonist John Coltrane said was his dream: "To be a force for good."

What Winfrey does and has been documented doing over the years is odd when we realize how different it would be were it being done by someone else. To bring it right down front, she throws some stuff in the game by taking her own brand of self-obsession and flipping it out of the lane where we witness an ever-increasing number of celebrities, half celebrities, and subtalents smashed onto our windshields by the electric flyswatters of media. We are well aware of what most of them are known for doing: nothing much other than basking in gossipy blather, walking down red carpets in absurd outfits, and spending their wealth at vulgar levels that mirror contemporary decadence in every possible way. That is why we have become irritated, disgusted, or feel demeaned by the overweening narcissism that delineates far too many of the wealthy and powerful. Then a curve ball, moving like a magical star, rises from Mississippi and takes its place in the firmament of public dreams and aspirations, showing us that an alternative sort of light is possible.

In explaining a painting by Goya to one of his wives, Picasso answered his own question of where the point of light came from: "Inside Goya himself." Oprah Winfrey is that way, internally illuminated as if she were actual architecture of a special sort. Architecture is about both the outside and the inside, as opposed to giving the false but convincing impression of an inside, like the movie sets that are all surface. While we have seen the surface form of Winfrey change many times over the years, the inside continues to expand, its depths increase, its understanding becoming almost epic in a way that drips not with glitter but with the inevitable charm that always arrives with deep feeling. The great Italian writer Roberto Calasso spends much of his time thinking and writing about how the act of literal or psychological seeing is what we tell one another about ourselves, or what we think those among whom we live happen to truly or possibly be.

Calasso is focused on the evolution of symbols that come to us in shifting forms over the centuries and are reassembled everywhere. Those are the mutations of meaning common to human experience. Calasso has an undaunted certainty in this evolution and assumes that what the great eighteenth-century painter Tiepolo always implied in his work was "I am, I shall be the one and the other." That amounts to a collective sense of narcissism. If we do not understand this unselfish narcissism, we cannot grasp Oprah Winfrey's achievement or understand the corkscrewing nature of its motion, which is particular to the American sense of universal destiny: E pluribus unum. Out of many, one. That is as close to equality as we presently understand it.

Easily the wealthiest and most powerful celebrity in the world, Winfrey has made another category for herself that is largely unprecedented. This woman's sense of herself and her obsessions remains profoundly unique. All that troubles or encourages Winfrey is what brought her out of the greasy woods and humid jungles of a celebrity that has no meaning other than profit and attention. To our astonishment, this queen of American goodwill goes far out of her way to make everything that she seeks for herself available to as many people as possible, wherever on this Earth they may live. I mean all of the people fighting on every level of the problems that make the planet go round and round or backward and backward. In an uncanny way, this child of Mississippi sees herself as a metaphor for human life at large, which is what each of us always is, one way or another. But few people have the power or the sensitivity to see their triumphs and their sorrows as representative of everything else that is going on, or is going off. Potential is unlimited in Winfrey's mind because of what happened with her and to her and what she attempts to make possible by her own actions. The sense of culture that she possesses is understandably complex, but her vision of race is very obvious, and that very obviousness has made her quite charismatic for more than twenty years. In her world, the only race, as the saying goes, is the human race. She does not just say it; she lives it and encourages others to live it as well.

Oprah Winfrey is far from naive and has been taken advantage of here and there, which is what happens to the high-minded among us. No one is incapable of being hustled, conned, or made a fool of right in front of everyone. That ongoing threat does not intimidate her. She has been in the storm so long that she expects to be knocked down, to be disappointed, to find out that someone or something she championed is far less than what she believed the person or the thing to be. What does she do about it? She lets the heartbreak happen and knows that it will heal in the open air where so much of her life is lived. We can all be sure that her best fighting weight is arrived at from working out in the ever-present heat of the kitchen, a broiling temperature all who intend to do good must learn to withstand. Solitude then meets glory. Consequently, her sense of equality is maintained through her integrity.

Freedom Riders

Oprah described the Freedom Riders as "young people rising up, willing to die for what they believed in. . . . If it were not for these American heroes, this country would be a very different place right now." She said that during "hate-filled and terrifying times in the South and other parts of the country, a fearless and determined group of Americans—men and women, black and white, many of them still in college at the time—joined together to fight against racial injustice in our country." They traveled to the segregated South and tested laws that prohibited segregation by riding in the front of buses and sitting in waiting rooms designated "whites only." Predictably, their actions were met with hostility and violence. "I don't want any niggers in here," was the usual response.

Janie Forsyth McKinney was only twelve when she witnessed the firebombing of a Freedom Riders' bus in front of her family's grocery store. Fourteen people were trapped inside the burning vehicle, and when they escaped, they were attacked by racists swinging baseball bats. But young Janie, confronted by the worst suffering she had ever seen, wanted to help. She walked into the crowd, washed a victim's face, and gave her water. Then she moved on to the next person, defying her neighbors. Local KKK members considered punishing her, but let her behavior pass because of her age. However, the appreciative Freedom Riders she helped that day, including Hank Thomas, called her a "little angel," a light in the darkness. Janie Forsyth McKinney and 178 survivors of the 1961 Freedom Rides reunited on Oprah's stage on May 4, 2011, to honor each other and the principles they struggled—at great personal cost—to uphold.

Oprah surrounded by 178
Freedom Riders, May 4, 2011.

Clockwise from top: Hank Thomas and Oprah;
Janie Forsyth McKinney and Oprah; Elwin Wilson,
John Lewis, and Oprah, May 4, 2011.

In 1996, more than thirty-five years after their brave fight to integrate Little Rock Central High School, seven of the nine black students who were known as the "Little Rock Nine" came to *The Oprah Winfrey Show* to meet three of their white tormentors face-to-face. It was a moving moment of healing and reconciliation as the contrite Southerners apologized for their behavior and asked for forgiveness. "I was raised in a racist family . . . and I'm sorry about that," said Ann Burleson, who was a teenager when she jeered at the black students as they tried to enter the school. Carlotta Walls LaNier, one of the "Nine," asked if she had broken that chain of bigotry with her own children. "That's what I've done right," Burleson answered affirmatively, offering a note of hope for future generations.

Many remarkable men and women who fought for equality sat beside Oprah on her stage, but one man stood apart from the others. "It is one of the greatest honors of my career to welcome Nelson Mandela," she announced in November of 2000, when the legendary South African leader and Nobel Peace Prize winner appeared on the show. Describing his release from prison as "a moment of incandescent joy," she asked the man who was considered to be the world's greatest leader some revelatory questions about his twenty-seven-year incarceration. "How is there no bitterness?" she wondered, marveling at Mandela's ability to work closely with his white oppressors after his release to build a new South Africa. He had to learn to make the brain dominate the blood, he told her, explaining how important it was for him to suppress his emotional response to his prison ordeal in order to achieve his larger goals of freedom and equality for blacks in South Africa. "Our emotions said, 'The white minority is an enemy. We must never talk with them.' But our brains said, 'If you don't talk with these men, your country will go up in flames. And for many years to come, this country would be engulfed in rivers of blood.'"

Oprah also pressed for insights about Mandela's personal story. She discussed his divorce from Winnie Mandela, his wife of thirty-four years, and his marriage, at the age of eighty, to Graça Machel, the widow of Mozambique's founding president, Samora

Top: Oprah greets Nelson Mandela, November 27, 2000.

Bottom: Nelson Mandela, Oprah, and the Harpo Studios staff, November 27, 2000.

Machel. "You say you are a man with weaknesses. Obviously, everybody has some. What are yours?" Oprah asked him. "So many, if I started telling you about them this would take the whole day," was his humble reply. To further illustrate Mandela's great humility, Oprah repeated a comment he made to a producer immediately before coming on stage. "What is the subject of today's show?" he asked innocently, and he seemed genuinely surprised when the producer answered "Nelson Mandela!" In an unprecedented demonstration of admiration, hundreds of Harpo employees lined the halls of the studio to applaud the great man. Subsequently, the corridor where they stood was named "The Nelson Mandela Hallway" in his honor.

In addition to celebrating icons and iconic moments of black history, *The Oprah Winfrey Show* examined contemporary, and frequently controversial, racial issues. Don Imus's deplorable description of a team of young African American women basketball players as "nappy-headed hos" prompted Oprah to ask, "After Imus, Now What?" She invited Maya Angelou; Stanley Crouch, a columnist for the New York *Daily News*; Jason Whitlock from the *Kansas City Star*; and Bruce Gordon, the former head of the NAACP, among others, to discuss that complicated question. The conversation led them to ask whether hip-hop culture has a negative effect on language and, more importantly, on the perception of African Americans.

Jason Whitlock argued, "We have allowed our kids to adopt a hip-hop culture that has been perverted and corrupted by prison values. They are defining our women in pop culture as 'bitches' and 'hos.'" Female students at Spelman College agreed with his analysis and said that they protested a performance by the rapper Nelly because of his misogynistic lyrics. But in a follow-up show, members of the rap community offered their own responses. Russell Simmons, chairman of the Hip-Hop Summit Action Network, emphasized that "The hip-hop community is a mirror, a reflection of the dirt we overlook— the violence, the misogyny, the sexism. . . . They need to be discussed."

Oprah debated the omnipresence of the "N" word in contemporary black culture with none other than superstar rapper Jay-Z, who defended its usage in rap music by arguing, "If we just start removing words from the dictionary, you just make up another word the next day. So we don't address the problem. The problem is racism, right? That's really the problem." Oprah disagreed, saying that she found the word denigrating. "When I hear the word," she explained, "I think about black men who were lynched and that was the last word they heard." Eventually, Oprah and Jay-Z agreed to disagree.

Racism wasn't the only equality battle Oprah set out to fight. In 1986, she hosted a show about homophobia, the first of more than two hundred addressing gay, lesbian,

Ellen DeGeneres

What If

Oprah Winfrey. We might not know that name if the civil rights movement hadn't happened in the sixties. It was widely accepted by society that "colored" people were not equal to "white" people. Throughout history, we've seen that certain groups of people—Jews, women, African Americans, homosexuals—were not thought to be of the same value, not equal. If things hadn't changed, if a few people hadn't risen up and spoken out and disagreed with the majority, if President Abraham Lincoln hadn't signed the Emancipation Proclamation and freed the slaves, the world would have missed out on so many brilliant minds—Oprah being one of them. Imagine a world without Martin Luther King, Jr., Maya Angelou, Stevie Wonder, architect Paul Williams, and George Washington Carver.

Oprah's show has been a beacon on television, a platform for education and spiritual awakening for millions of people every day. Oprah has opened up a world of examples of love and nonjudgment. We have watched people survive tragic events, overcome great losses, and all the while she has been our teacher for hope and open-mindedness. And the light that is Oprah, the brilliant mind that is Oprah, might never have been because of the color of her skin.

Unfortunately, the judgment and prejudice toward homosexuals continue today. Gays and lesbians do not have equal rights. We are still widely seen as second-class citizens.

We are all of equal value—not the same value—but equal. Every life-form on Earth comes from the same source—God, or whatever name you give our creator. This creator, God, made all of us, every living thing.

Ants can lift ten times their body weight. I can't do that, and yet I'm considered more powerful. Everything in life is relative. We all have different talents. Dolphins, whales, and bats have sonar—a type of hearing that enables them to know their surroundings by sound, not by sight. Dogs can hear a frequency that we can't. Who's to say what's more valuable, what's expendable?

If you really look at nature, it's all equally important. Nothing goes to waste. Everything is in perfect balance. It's man who decides to genetically engineer corn so that bugs won't eat it. Then what happens to the bugs that can't eat? And then what happens to the birds that can't eat the bugs? When we decide that something has more, or less, value, we throw everything off balance.

When I think about equality, I think about all of life. I look at a tree that's one hundred years old and appreciate its beauty, its endurance. I know that it was once an acorn that seemed small and insignificant. There is value and potential in everything—even the smallest things are here for a reason and contribute to the circle of life.

It seems to me that just as each fingerprint is unique—that no two people share the same one—each life is unique in its purpose and our journey is uniquely our own. For anyone to judge or decide that someone is better than, greater than, or has more value than someone else is arrogant and ignorant. We didn't create this world; we are temporarily living here—we are tenants on this extraordinary planet called Earth. Equality to me means all things are equally important and all life is to be respected and protected and appreciated. It's not a man or woman thing; a black or white or Latina or Asian or Muslim thing. It's not a heterosexual or homosexual thing. It's a precious gift of life. It's rising up high above Earth and looking down and seeing how equally expendable we all are.

This planet goes on with or without us. As the custodians of this planet, let's try to respect it and all things that live here.

and transgender issues during the past twenty-five years. "When it comes to controversial subjects, we've always tried to face them head on," Oprah said. Considering that in 1987, "Nearly 70% of all Americans think homosexual behavior is sinful," according to the *Los Angeles Times*, the subject wasn't just controversial; it was explosive. But *The Oprah Winfrey Show* was committed to promoting understanding, one viewer, one mind, one heart at a time. "Our intention is and has always been to help people see things differently by giving a voice to those who might not otherwise be heard," she said.

In 1987, Oprah brought her microphone to Williamson, West Virginia, where she covered a story about a prejudice born of ignorance, anger, and fear. One hot day in July, a young man named Mike Sisco jumped into the town swimming pool to cool off. When the swimmers around him realized he was in their midst, "they kind of ran like people do on science-fiction movies where Godzilla walks into the street," Sisco later recalled. He was a homosexual who had been diagnosed with AIDS, so the sight of him in the communal water caused everyone to panic. The mayor closed the pool to ward off infection, and Sisco was treated like a pariah, shunned and reviled.

As Oprah had done in Forsyth County and Los Angeles, she invited members of the community to a town meeting to express their feelings about the swimming-pool incident and its aftermath. Her only agenda that day was to banish ignorance and promote compassion. The townspeople gathered to discuss their knowledge of AIDS, which consisted mostly of misconceptions, and their feelings about homosexuality, which were hostile. By the end of the broadcast, the group was more educated about the virus and the plight of their unfortunate neighbor who suffered from it. Some people maintained that they were "repulsed" by Mike Sisco's lifestyle and held firm to their prejudices, but those who listened to the discussion and processed the information they heard felt the first stirrings of awareness and acceptance. Oprah believed that her most significant contribution to the AIDS crisis was "to tell the stories of the people who had AIDS and to humanize that story so that other people

Oprah and Mike Sisco, November 16, 1987.

would understand that this could be my brother . . . this could be my father . . . this could be my sister . . . this could be my mother . . . this could be my aunt . . . and that there, but for the grace of God, that could be me."

The Oprah Winfrey Show continued to host shows dedicated to demystifying homosexuality. "Are you born gay?" Oprah asked. "When did you know that you were gay?" "Should gay marriages be legalized?" Her questions—and her guests' candid answers—served the dual purpose of educating viewers and making homosexuality less threatening. The *Advocate* called *The Oprah Winfrey Show* "a national town hall for rational discussion about gay and lesbian issues." Through Oprah, viewers became familiar with gays, lesbians, bisexuals, and transgenders—individuals who might not be a part of their everyday lives. Eventually, people who once seemed so "different," so alien, emerged as fellow human beings on a very human quest for happiness and fulfillment.

The Oprah Winfrey Show also provided a safe and welcoming environment where gay men and women could "come out." On October 11, 1988, the date designated as "National Coming Out Day," members of

Greg Louganis surprises
Michael, January 25, 2011.

Oprah's audience courageously stood onstage to announce their true identity to the world. "My name is Juanita and I want to tell my family and friends that I'm gay," said one participant. "Hello America, I'm gay," a young man declared proudly. With Oprah supporting them, they were unafraid of speaking out.

In 1995, Olympic diver Greg Louganis joined the ranks of Oprah's "outs" when he appeared on the show to speak publicly for the first time about being gay and HIV positive. In an emotional interview, he told Oprah that when he was living in the shadow of his secret, he preferred to stay home alone with his dogs because, "If I was out in public, then I had to edit myself. I was feeling like a fake and also I was feeling, how could anybody accept me if they knew me?" Louganis's heart-piercing honesty made an impression on a twelve-year-old boy named Michael, who was watching the show that day and struggling with his own fears about coming out. Louganis inspired him to be himself: to live openly and with pride. Sixteen years later, Oprah arranged a surprise on-air meeting for Michael and his hero.

In 1997, when Ellen DeGeneres wanted to speak openly about her famous coming out—her *TIME* magazine, "Yep, I'm gay" moment—she sat down with Oprah (who also played her therapist on *Ellen* when her character debated whether or not to come out). Ellen answered Oprah's questions, both serious and playful ("When did you know that you were gay? Was it something like bing, bing, bing, bing, bing, gay bells go off?"), and bantered good-naturedly with audience members, whether they expressed disapproval or support. She admitted that at one time she worried that Oprah wouldn't like her if she knew she were gay. But now she was more confident about her sexuality. "I'm fine with who I am. I feel good about me," she said.

Chastity Bono echoed these sentiments when she appeared on *The Oprah Winfrey Show* in 1998 to discuss her much-publicized "outing" as a lesbian. She and her mother, Cher, talked to Oprah about the process of a family's coming to terms with a child's homosexuality. Thirteen years later, in 2011, Bono was back on the show to discuss a surprising

new development in her life: This time the subject was transgenderism. Chastity had transitioned from female to male and was now known as Chaz. When he was a "she," Chaz told Oprah during a landmark interview, he always felt as if he were trapped in the wrong body. "As early as I have memory and consciousness, I felt like a boy," he said. *Oprah* had featured other stories about transgenders, but this was the most public one. After listening to Chaz, viewers were better equipped—and perhaps more inclined—to see him as a *person.*

Religion was another hot topic that *The Oprah Winfrey Show* addressed head on. In 2001, a few weeks after the September 11 attacks, Oprah hosted a show called "Islam 101." "We're calling this program 'Islam 101' because we're figuring that a lot of you all, just like those of us working here at the *Oprah* show, don't know even the basics," she explained. At that moment, Islam was a sensitive subject for most Americans because they were afraid of the unknowns, but Oprah wanted to enlighten her viewers and encourage them to use what they learned to progress "beyond tolerance, which really implies that we're just putting up with you, but we don't really like you," to genuine understanding. The *New York Times* congratulated her for "demystifying Islam and going past the knee-jerk pleas against discrimination that have been so much a part of the pop-cultural conversation. The magic of Ms. Winfrey's approach is to be blatantly educational without being condescending."

The Oprah Winfrey Show's ongoing mission to provide the misunderstood, the silenced, and the oppressed with a voice even included animals, who, of course, could not speak for themselves. "I believe that how we treat the least of beings among us determines our own humanity," Oprah stated on the show "Lisa Ling Reports: How We Treat the Animals We Eat," which covered the debate concerning farm animals and their right to inhabit more space. "This November in California, voters are going to be asked to weigh in on a measure called Proposition 2," she reported in 2008. "That proposition calls for egg-laying hens, pregnant pigs, and veal calves to be able to stand up, to be able to

Oprah discusses Islam with Professor Akbar Ahmed of American University in an effort to enlighten viewers about what the Islamic religion both is and is not, October 5, 2001.

lie down, to be able to fully extend their limbs without touching the side of an enclosure." Oprah wanted her viewers to be informed about the issue because she believed that animals, even those who were destined for the dinner table, were entitled to a better life. The animal-rights organization PETA announced Oprah as its 2008 Person of the Year, commending her for using her fame to "help the less fortunate, including animals."

Season after season, viewers witnessed positive stories about people who were discriminated against on the basis of race, sexual preference, gender, age, religion, physical condition, appearance, and a myriad of other prejudices invented by man. Gradually, through exposure and education, Oprah's viewers learned to look beyond these superficial differences to find their shared humanity— the first step toward effecting change. Today, previously all-white Forsyth County has thousands of African American residents and is considered a great place to live and raise a family. Jim Rainey, the racist who learned to love his biracial grandson, returned to the show to share the news that he had adopted two African American boys. "These are my

boys, my sons, Robert and Walter," he said. "I hope that . . . I . . . last long enough to see them raised and have opportunities—the opportunities that thugs like me would have denied them forty years ago." And now, farm animals in California will experience more humane treatment because voters in that state approved Proposition 2.

For twenty-five years, *The Oprah Winfrey Show* has been a powerful and vigilant force in the fight for equality. At the start of each show, before any prejudices were exposed, injustices righted, historic events commemorated, or issues debated, it was Oprah Winfrey herself who shattered every senseless stereotype regarding race, gender, class, and anything else. The second she walked onstage, she was living proof that barriers could be crossed and opportunities realized. Oprah had a voice like no other. If she embraced a person or a cause, her viewers were likely to do the same. The fact that an African American woman (a member of two groups with a long history of oppression) was invited into millions of homes every day as a trusted, even beloved, friend opened the door for others to follow.

Speaking "Out" on *Oprah*

The Oprah Winfrey Show is the proud recipient of eight GLAAD Media Awards for Outstanding Talk Show Episode. Oprah's commitment to promoting acceptance for gay and transgender people was evident on the award-winning shows "Ricky Martin Coming Out as a Gay Man and a New Dad" (for 2010); "Ellen DeGeneres and Her Wife, Portia de Rossi" (for 2009); "Born in the Wrong Body" (for 2007); "Wives Confess They Are Gay" (for 2006); "When I Knew I was Gay" (for 2005); "The 11-Year-Old Who Wants a Sex Change" (for 2004); "The Husband Who Became a Woman" (for 2003); and "Ellen's Coming Out" (for 1997). These topics were often challenging for both guests and viewers, but Oprah approached each show, no matter how controversial, with an intention. "I want the world to know how we are all really more alike than we are differ-ent. And so if the message of that, in any myriad of ways that we can express it every day, gets across to the millions of people who see us in this country and around the world, then I feel like then I would have done my job," she said.

Oprah's efforts to enlighten her audience about transgender people were particularly ground-breaking. When she introduced women who had become men, and men who had become women, and explored their stories, she helped viewers to understand that their desire to change their bodies was a matter of *identity*, not sexuality—that it was possible for a person to know very early in life that he or she had been born in the wrong body. "Would I have the courage to do what these people are getting ready to do today?" she asked before bringing on guests who had transgendered. She respected their choices, honored their stories, treated them with her signature blend of humanity and humor—and encouraged everyone watching to do the same.

GLAAD bid *Oprah* a fond farewell in May 2011, writing, "GLAAD sends our heartfelt congratula-tions on 25 remarkable years of *The Oprah Winfrey Show*. We thank you, and your team at Harpo Studios, for a quarter century of unwavering dedication to telling the stories of LGBT people from around the world."

Clockwise from top left: Parents Eric and Karen, along with nine-year-old Hal, a transgender boy who was formerly a girl named Hallie, May 12, 2004; Oprah and eleven-year-old Kaden, a transgender boy who was formerly a girl named Kayla, May 12, 2004; Jenny Boylan talks about the transition from husband and father to woman, May 6, 2003.

Clockwise from bottom left: Portia de Rossi and Ellen DeGeneres discuss their relationship, November 9, 2011; Joe and Chris, formerly married, both of whom now identify as gay, October 2, 2006; Carson Kressley, Billy Porter, and Robert Trachtenberg discuss when they first realized they were gay and how they told their families, November 17, 2005.

Henry Louis Gates, Jr.

Why Oprah Is Oprah

One day in 1978 my phone rang. I was a junior professor at Yale, trying to establish a family and trying to get tenure, and I wasn't watching much TV. It was my mother. "Skippy," Mom began. "There is something you need to know about." Knowing about my intellectual interest in and passion for black culture, my parents were always trying to alert me to things emerging in our culture that I should know about. But I had never heard so much excitement in my mother's voice.

"People are talking," my mother said.

"Talking about what?"

"No, silly, that's the name of this great program out of Baltimore on WJZ-TV. It's called *People Are Talking*. And it is hosted by this great colored woman. Her name is Oprah."

"Oprah? What kind of name is that?"

"I don't know," Mom said. "But that's her name. Oprah Winfrey. Your father says it's from the Bible. Anyway, who cares? She's a genius and you have got to watch her!"

"Uh-huh . . . Mom, I'm too busy to watch television. What I got to do is write my PhD thesis and get tenure."

Always trust your mom.

Actor, entrepreneur, philanthropist, literary tastemaker, Oprah Winfrey is an American phenomenon whose own intellectual depth, curiosity about the world in which we live and the history of the diverse civilizations that have helped to make our world, cosmopolitan empathy, and relentless generosity have influenced millions around the globe. I am most fortunate to count myself among those millions. It is common to speak of a person as a force of nature, and Miss Winfrey would most certainly qualify for that designation. But I think of her as a force of culture, a force of civilization itself.

Oprah's good works have already become the stuff of legend. And even a partial list is long. Oprah's Angel Network has generated millions of dollars in donations to establish sixty new schools in thirteen countries, including the Oprah Winfrey Leadership Academy for Girls in South Africa (the opening of which I had the pleasure of attending, an experience somewhat akin to witnessing the founding of Eton or Exeter on the African continent) and Seven Fountains, a coed primary school serving one thousand students in KwaZulu-Natal province. Oprah's group has also helped to build and restore homes destroyed in the Gulf region by Hurricane Katrina, supported women living with HIV/AIDS in numerous African communities, and battled hunger in urban communities in Washington, D.C., and near Chicago—to name just a few of the areas of her philanthropic organization's impact. There never has been a more generous humanitarian in the history of the African and African American people, and that is an honor rarely noted about Miss Winfrey.

Oprah's philanthropy is driven by the philosophy that each of us has it within ourselves to do better, to do more, to affect our communities in positive ways. Through her own drive and discipline, she has built what can certainly be called an entertainment empire, one that reaches into television, radio, publishing, and the Internet. Drawing, perhaps, on a long family tradition of business acumen and entrepreneurship, Oprah has as much business savvy as any of my colleagues or their students at the Harvard Business School! But she has also engineered and executed a model of business that both works and gives back extraordinarily, one in which personal wealth must be used for the greater good of the community.

It has often been said that Oprah's influence has a certain gurulike quality to it. If Oprah likes a book, its sales increase thousandsfold; if Oprah likes a particular handbag, we see it on the arms of countless women around the country. There is a great deal to be said for this type of influence, especially as it relates to Oprah's philanthropic efforts and especially to what can only be called her formation of a new reading public. She has accomplished for writers and publishers what no critic in the *New York Times* or the *New York Review of Books* has done or could possibly do: She has created an appetite for reading books in a postmodern, highly technological culture whose attention span and intellectual discipline seem otherwise to diminish by the day, rivaled as they are by ever-faster media and PDAs. Oprah embodies the ultimate paradox: She is a television star who has gotten people to turn off the TV, to open books and read. I see this accomplishment as very much in line with her philanthropic work: She has an unrivaled ability to get people to open their hearts and minds and invest in their communities and in their world.

It has been one of my greatest experiences of the past few years to get to know Oprah. When she agreed to be a subject for my 2006 PBS documentary, *African American Lives*, I knew—and appreciated the fact—that her involvement would add a particular luster to the program and that it would garner attention from an audience that I might not otherwise reach as easily, especially on public television. However, I had no idea that her participation would add such depth to the program. What we learned through state-of-the-art DNA analysis and old-fashioned historical research and genealogical sleuthing in the course of our investigation of her roots was astounding.

Her people were, not surprisingly, slaves, but what they did once out of slavery was rare and nothing short of phenomenal. We found her great-great-grandparents, Constantine and Violet Winfrey, living in Attala County in Mississippi in the 1870 census. They were, like almost all slaves, illiterate. Six years later, in 1876—the year that Reconstruction ended—this same great-great-grandfather walked up to a white man—a Confederate veteran named James Watson—and made a bargain, the proverbial deal with the Devil. If Constantine picked, on his own time, eight bales of clean or "lint" cotton, and gave that cotton to Watson, he would in turn give the Winfreys eighty acres of prime bottom land, with a creek running through it and surrounded by gently rolling hills. Eight bales of cotton weigh 3,200 pounds. Now, that is a lot of cotton! The white man must have thought this former slave crazy, but he struck a deal. But if the total poundage was even one ounce short, the white man kept all the cotton and the land. Classic deal with the Devil, right? Destined to fail, right?

Wrong! I handed Oprah the deed to the land signed by Mr. Watson's son and wife, dated 1881, and signed by none other than Constantine Winfrey himself! He and Violet had not only worked ceaselessly to buy eighty acres of land just as Reconstruction was ending and the Klan was coming into its own, but he had learned to read and write as well! And on that land in rural Mississippi, where Redemption kept blacks in thrall to whites for years after Emancipation and Reconstruction, he built a school for the colored children in his community. Do you want to know why Oprah Winfrey is Oprah Winfrey? Ask Constantine and Violet.

Oprah's reaction to the revelation of this history of education as well as to her maternal genetic roots in the Kpelle people of Liberia revealed so much about what we carry of our ancestors, how we work to honor them, and how we understand who we are and where we are going by understanding where we come from.

It is my great pleasure and privilege to call this truly outstanding individual a friend; I am indeed honored to know someone who has done so much for the world around her, and whose generosity and capacity for learning and teaching show no signs of slowing, even as she moves on to this next stage of her career. In Japan, when a great person reaches the age of sixty, they are declared a national treasure. We have no such equivalent in the United States. But if the United Nations undertook such a task, there is no doubt in my mind that Oprah Winfrey would be declared one of the world's first international treasures. And it was my mother, way back in 1978, who was among the first to predict this young woman's dazzling future.

Predictions are always risky matters, of course, but I believe that when the history of our era is written, and the list of those geniuses who sensed the zeitgeist, along with the names of Bill Gates, Steve Jobs, and Mark Zuckerberg, will stand the name of Oprah Winfrey.

Giving Back

"Everybody can be great, because everybody can serve."

–Dr. Martin Luther King, Jr.

She also realized that she could use her platform to inspire others to give, thereby building an army of everyday philanthropists who would have a powerful and far-reaching impact on the world.

Oprah launches
the Angel Network,
September 18, 1997.

People often have philanthropic impulses, but no idea how to act on them. They believe it takes the bank account of a Bill Gates, or the selfless dedication of a Mother Teresa, to make a meaningful contribution. They worry about choosing the right cause when there are so many, or convince themselves that in tough times, charity begins at home. And sometimes they fall victim to what spiritual advisor Marianne Williamson calls the "I care, therefore I don't have to do anything" syndrome—the misconception that *feeling* obviates the need for *doing*.

The Oprah Winfrey Show's mission was to teach viewers that "caring" is a verb, and Oprah herself assumed a leadership position in that initiative. When she first started making money, her dream was to pass it on, and she did. However, she also realized that she could use her platform to inspire others to give, thereby building an army of everyday philanthropists who would have a powerful and far-reaching impact on the world.

Oprah believed that television was a way of opening people's hearts, and she frequently featured guests whose stories demonstrated the power of giving. In 1994, eight-year-old Nora Gross described the genesis of the "Penny Harvest" to Oprah and her audience. When she was four years old, Nora saw a homeless man in her neighborhood and asked her father if they could take him home. Wanting to cultivate her generous impulse, her father suggested that she collect spare change—pennies essentially—to donate to organizations that served the needy. They raised $1,000 at the time and founded what went on to become the largest child-philanthropy program in the United States.

Nora inspired generations of children to collect pennies that funded millions of dollars worth of good deeds, and she also inspired Oprah, who started thinking about how small change could lead to big change. They envisioned an imaginary piggy bank that stretched from one end of America to the other, filled with the forgotten coins that were buried in purses, pockets, backpacks, jars, junk drawers, and sofas. What if *The Oprah Winfrey Show* dispatched volunteers to collect all that money and put it to good use, just like Nora Gross? "Well," Oprah thought, "if she's just a

little girl who could do that, I wonder what we can do? I've got a big old TV show."

That piggy bank sprouted wings and evolved into the public charity known as Oprah's Angel Network. It took flight on September 18, 1997, when Oprah invited her audience to work with her to achieve identifiable goals—such as collecting pennies—that would improve the lives of others. "I'm planning to commit myself, and I hope you'll join me in making a difference by using your time—whatever time you have, whatever talents you have, and most of all, our hearts," to get the job done.

There were five specific things people could do *right now* to make a difference: gather up that spare change to send kids to college; volunteer to build an Oprah Habitat for Humanity home; offer to do a job for free for someone who really needed the help; volunteer at school; and create a mini-miracle for others whenever there was an opportunity to do so.

Viewers immediately answered Oprah's call to action. In a little over a year, the coins collected by kids, organizations, and even President Bill Clinton and First Lady Hillary Clinton in the White House, added up to a whopping $3,557,083.94 in change, enough money to provide 150 students with $25,000 scholarships. People who never held a hammer or a paintbrush signed on to build two hundred homes for needy families across America. A mechanic volunteered to repair cars for single mothers, while a piano teacher gave free lessons to students who couldn't afford to pay for them. As Oprah suspected, people cared about one another—they just needed a little help determining how to express that concern.

Donations poured in, enabling the Angel Network to distribute funds to hundreds of organizations throughout the United States and in more than thirty countries around the globe. In 1999, social activist Craig Keilburger appeared on *Oprah* to talk about Free the Children, the organization he founded when he was twelve years old. An impassioned Keilburger, now sixteen, was on a mission to get children to help children through education. He wanted to raise money to build schools in third world countries. Oprah shocked him by spontaneously offering to donate, and the look of amazement and joy on Keilburger's

Nicholas Kristof

Oprah's Gift

Oprah Winfrey is one of the most powerful women in the world, with one of the mightiest podiums. And some of the least powerful, most voiceless women and girls in the world are those in Africa with a devastating childbirth injury called a fistula. Simply put, women with fistulas are the opposite of Oprah.

A fistula typically happens to a young teenage girl, with a pelvis not yet fully formed, too young to give birth. There is no doctor around, the baby gets stuck and eventually dies, and the girl is left with a hole between her vagina and bladder or rectum. She becomes incontinent, leaking waste nonstop through her vagina. Acid from the dribbling urine leaves ulcers on her legs. She stinks and leaves puddles of urine everywhere she goes and every time she wakes from a nap. Her husband abandons her, her community scorns her as filthy, and she becomes a pariah. A hut is built for her at the edge of the village, downwind from the other huts, and she may be barred from using the village well. She thinks she has been cursed by God, she suffers from infections, and she may kill herself.

Yet there's an easy repair for a fistula. It was devised by an American ob-gyn in the nineteenth century, when many American women suffered from the same condition. Indeed, there was a fistula hospital in New York City (where the Waldorf-Astoria Hotel is today) in the late nineteenth and early twentieth centuries. But as more American women gained access to doctors and C-sections, fistulas became extremely rare in America—and people in the West stopped thinking about them, even though millions of African and Asian women continued to suffer from them.

The center of treatment in Africa has been an extraordinary hospital in Addis Ababa, the capital of Ethiopia, called the Addis Ababa Fistula Hospital. Founded by an Australian doctor, Catherine Hamlin, it repairs fistulas at a cost of about $400 each. But the hospital was struggling to raise funds to meet its expenses. Dr. Hamlin was a Mother Teresa–like figure, but unknown to the world.

Then along came Oprah. Her team saw an article I had written about Dr. Hamlin, and even though it concerned an esoteric and unpleasant problem halfway around the world, she resolved to have Dr. Hamlin on her show. The team flew Dr. Hamlin from Ethiopia to Chicago, and the audience heard an extraordinary discussion that could not have been more distant from standard television fare: a program about holes in the vaginas of the most voiceless women in the world.

When the show aired, it transformed the problem of fistula. Women from around America, even the world, were appalled to learn of such a devastating injury that could be so easily repaired. They wrote checks that permanently changed the prospects of the Addis Ababa Fistula Hospital, allowing it to open branches around Ethiopia and perform surgeries abroad.

Oprah followed up by traveling to Ethiopia to film a show, and she also personally donated funds for a new wing of the hospital. Television viewers embraced the cause, and fistulas went from being unmentionable to becoming a pressing problem that deserved urgent action. Today there are three American charities focused on fistula, and many others support fistula patients. The United States government and the United Nations both help fistula patients.

What made the difference was that Oprah lent her voice to those who had none. Americans by and large want to help, but they worry about corruption and other obstacles. So when someone they trust tells them on television that this is a problem that can be fixed, they respond with unbelievable enthusiasm. I've seen that over and over.

In 2009, my wife, Sheryl WuDunn, and I published a book arguing that the greatest moral challenge of our time is addressing the oppression that is the lot of so many women around the world. The book, called *Half the Sky*, received fabulous reviews, but had trouble getting television time because executive producers saw it as about distant people—the world's poor don't watch network television. Better to put a Democrat and a Republican in a studio and have them yell at each other—that'll get ratings up!

The Oprah Winfrey Show more than made up for the omissions elsewhere, with two full shows devoted to the book. Oprah threw herself into the planning, even sending a camera crew all the way to Zimbabwe to tell a story from the book that she found particularly moving; the story of a woman named Tererai Trent who had grown up herding cattle and who was denied a chance to go to school. Tererai studied on her own, and, after a visit from an American aid worker, wrote down goals on a piece of paper: She would study in America, earn an undergraduate degree, a master's degree, and even a PhD. Tererai wrapped the paper in plastic and buried it in an old can in a field. Over the years, Tererai had the chance to study in the United States and earn her degrees, and each time she returned to Zimbabwe, she would dig up the can and check off her accomplishments. In 2009, she finally earned her PhD and became Dr. Trent.

For me, the shows underscored not only Oprah's passion for using her podium to do good, but also her shrewdness as a TV executive. I'm a *New York Times* columnist and live in the media world, but Oprah intuitively possesses some of the best storytelling skills that I've ever seen. She knew that she could engage an audience with the challenges of global female illiteracy—but that the way to do it was with a riveting and hopeful story such as Tererai Trent's. And Oprah also insisted that there be links on her website for her viewers to donate and make a difference. These were not general contributions to organizations, but donations for specific needs such as a safe-birthing kit in West Africa or a girl's education in Zambia.

No surprise—Oprah was exactly right. Viewers responded with a torrent of donations, and all around Africa today there are girls who got an education or gave birth safely because of *The Oprah Winfrey Show*, even if they've never heard of it. Oprah simultaneously respected her audience's intelligence, appealed to the better angels of its nature, and engaged it with riveting material— a trifecta. That mix of softhearted compassion and hardheaded media brilliance is what gives Oprah Winfrey such an impact in so many places. And that's why one of her legacies is not just her show, but also that teenage African girls who find themselves leaking waste are no longer as likely to be shunted off forever to a hut at the edge of their village. Rather, they can get a modest surgery to repair a fistula and live out their lives with dignity, contributing to a better world. Saving the lives of people who have never heard of you may be the richest legacy of all

face illustrated the adage that giving is its own reward. Together, the Angel Network and Free the Children built more than fifty-five schools in twelve countries.

The Angel Network also teamed with Free the Children to launch O Ambassadors, a school-based program created to inspire young people to become active, compassionate, and knowledgeable global citizens. The inaugural group of O Ambassadors was comprised of twelve students with diverse backgrounds from various parts of North America. When they learned that they could build a school in Kenya for about $8,500, they organized fund-raisers—from dodgeball tournaments to school carnivals to kissing booths—eventually raising the money and heading off to Africa to get to work. Their three-week trip to Kenya, a time spent getting to know the people and customs of Elerai, the village where they built the school, was a life-changing experience for these young social activists.

In 2000, the Angel Network introduced the Use Your Life Awards to honor more than fifty "Good Samaritan" organizations and their founders. Donna Carson opened My House, a home for babies born to drug-addicted mothers. Lynn Price welcomed siblings who were separated by foster care to reunite during the summer at Camp to Belong. And Bonnie Begin started a program enabling troubled teens to find a better path in life by training assist dogs. The Angel Network gave them the resources they needed to continue their good works.

In addition to recognizing organizations for their humanitarian work, *The Oprah Winfrey Show* celebrated individuals who quietly "gave back." Fannie Eugene, a beloved housekeeper and nanny in New Orleans, took in her nephew and two nieces when her sister died. Her door was never closed to the people she loved. "Fannie Eugene makes the world a better place for everybody who comes in touch with her," wrote her admiring employer, who added, "She is the best person I know. If ever in this entire world there is a person who is deserving of a dream to come true, it's Fannie Eugene, my best friend." In 2003, Oprah paid tribute to what she called Fannie's "live to give" spirit by flying her to Chicago, placing a tiara

Left: Oprah reunites Clemantine (center, back row) and Claire Wamariya (third from right) with the rest of their family from Rwanda, in an episode featuring Elie Wiesel, May 25, 2006.

Right: Tiffany Tant (right) received $1,000 as part of Oprah's "Pay It Forward Challenge." First-grade teacher Alesia Hamilton (left) suggested she use the money to buy one of her students, sixty-eight-year-old Alferd Williams (middle), his own library of books, November 27, 2006.

Opposite, top: Oprah with the first O Ambassadors, May 26, 2008.

Opposite, middle: As "Princess for a Day," Fannie Eugene is given housecleaning services every week for a year, a trip to New York, and a van, February 17, 2003.

Opposite, bottom: Laurie Mullick, a teacher in Chicago, is surprised with an entire wardrobe from Dana Buchman and shoes from Stuart Weitzman, February 17, 2003.

on her head, and proclaiming her "Princess for a Day." Fannie was also given a brand-new van for her expanded family.

She had no idea that her prized van would be a lifesaver. When Hurricane Katrina hit in 2005, Fannie piled her family into the van and headed for safety, wearing her tiara the whole time. Her home was destroyed by the storm, but *The Oprah Winfrey Show* stepped in with a brand-new house designed and furnished by Nate Berkus. Knowing that the Eugenes would always extend a helping hand to others, Nate made sure to include plenty of room to accommodate Princess Fannie's guests.

One of the abiding lessons on *The Oprah Winfrey Show* was that the true value of giving is the way it makes both the giver and the recipient feel. An act of kindness reminds everyone that wonderful things can happen in life. Clemantine and Claire Wamariya were little girls growing up in Rwanda when, in 1994, their country suffered one of the bloodiest genocides in history. They managed to survive the massacre that claimed eight hundred thousand lives by hiding in a banana tree, but they believed their family had been slain. Eventually, in 2000, they moved to America, and after years of searching for news of their relatives—hoping that they had somehow survived—the sisters were thrilled to learn that their parents were alive, though completely out of reach, on the other side of the world.

When Oprah's Book Club held an essay contest in 2006 in conjunction with Elie Wiesel's Holocaust memoir, *Night*, Clemantine, by then a high school student, submitted a winning piece about her experiences in Rwanda. She and Claire were invited to appear on the show with Wiesel and the essay winners. At one point during the show, Oprah called the sisters to the stage to give them a surprise—a letter from their parents, whom they had not seen for twelve years. But Oprah said they didn't need to read it because their family was there, *in person*, at that very moment. She had flown their parents and younger siblings (a brother and a sister they had never met) to Chicago. The Wamariyas walked onstage, the most meaningful gift the girls could ever hope to receive. "There are a few times over the past twenty-five years when I can say that I witnessed a miracle on this show," Oprah said. "This is one of those times."

Oprah found a unique way to combine caring and sharing later that year when she hosted the "Pay It Forward Challenge." Instead of giving the studio audience a selection of her Favorite Things for the holiday season— a coveted assortment of garments, gadgets, and other items handpicked by Oprah herself— she gave them what she called "the gift of giving back." Each person in the audience— more than three hundred—received $1,000 and the "challenge" to come up with inspiring

Use Your Life Awards

Oprah's Angel Network introduced the Use Your Life Award on *The Oprah Winfrey Show* in 2000, when Valdimir Joseph, founder of the organization Inner Strength, was recognized for his mentoring program for young people. Inner Strength offered disadvantaged inner-city students the help they needed—including tutoring and GED prep, SAT prep, general high school studies, mentoring in life skills, wellness management, and violence prevention—to rise above their circumstances. Inner Strength used Oprah's Angel Network Use Your Life Award money to renovate a new space, purchase a passenger van for after-school programs and field trips, and fund a summer program on the campus of Morehouse College.

Over the next three years, Oprah recognized more than fifty life-changing organizations dedicated to improving their local communities. They usually began as someone's good idea, or even just a good deed, and blossomed into a full-fledged program. Police officer Julia Burney-Witherspoon distributed books to the children on her beat (Cops 'n Kids); Bea Salazar found a child foraging for food in a dumpster, took him home, made him a peanut butter and jelly sandwich, and founded Bea's Kids, a social-services program for underserved children in Texas; Irasema Salcido, the daughter of migrant farmworkers, earned an MA in Education from Harvard and then opened the Cesar Chavez High School for other kids with dreams; Rafe Esquith used his passion for Shakespeare to transform inner-city children at Hobart Elementary School in central Los Angeles into scholars; and, through Operation HOPE, John Bryant helped inner-city families get the financial education they needed to obtain loans, start businesses, and become homeowners. "Pass it on," Oprah encouraged the Use Your Life Award winners, which they did, and continue to do today.

Clockwise from top: Richard ("Benny") Bienvenue, founder of Our House, Inc., a program where at-risk young men learn the trade of carpentry and other life skills while getting their high school diplomas, August 28, 2000; Police Officer Julia Burney-Witherspoon started Cops 'n Kids, a reading program where police officers distribute books to children, September 25, 2000; Dr. Joseph Marshall accepts a Use Your Life Award for his Omega Boys Club, which gets teens off the street and into college, June 25, 2001.

and creative ways to use the money to help others. They were given a camera to document their good deeds and told that they had one week to get the job done.

The race was on to "pay it forward," and Oprah's philanthropists-in-training outdid themselves in accomplishing that goal. A woman from Illinois used her money to help a man who couldn't support his family because he had a neurological disorder. The whole town worked with her to raise money, growing her initial $1,000 to more than $70,000.

Kasey Osborne and Kristy O'Connor decided to donate their money to My Sister's House, a battered-women's shelter in Chicago. But they didn't stop there. They called retailers, made appeals on the radio, and convinced local supermarkets to offer customers the option of "paying it forward" on their grocery bill, rounding up the total to the nearest dollar and giving that money to the shelter. Even Oprah was impressed by the results. In one week, Osborne and O'Connor raised more than $200,000 for My Sister's House. Tiffany Tant placed a notice in her local newspaper asking people to nominate a person who deserved her $1,000. First-grade teacher Alesia Hamilton suggested sixty-eight-year-old Alferd Williams, a man she had taught to read and who was an honorary student in her class. Using Tant's money, Hamilton gave Williams his very own library. The pay it forward choices were inspired and inspiring. And, just as Oprah hoped, the people who participated felt so happy and fulfilled by their efforts that they truly understood—some for the first time— that it *is* better to give.

The Oprah Winfrey Show succeeded in opening viewers' eyes, hearts, and sometimes wallets to issues that were unfamiliar and that affected people in faraway places, such as Africa. Oprah herself resisted running a story on the little-known problem called "obstetric fistula"—a condition that occurs in young girls who are married and impregnated when their bodies are immature. During childbirth, the pressure sometimes causes a hole between the bladder and the vagina, or the rectum and the vagina— a fistula that can leak urine or feces. The afflicted girls are considered unclean by their communities and treated as outcasts, essentially ending their young lives before they have started.

Bono and Oprah go shopping for (RED) products on Michigan Avenue in Chicago to raise money to fight AIDS, October 13, 2006.

Opposite: Oprah visits Dr. Catherine Hamlin, who has provided free reconstructive surgery to more than twenty-five thousand African girls and women suffering from fistulas at the Addis Ababa Fistula Hospital in Ethiopia, which she opened with her late husband, Reginald, December 1, 2005.

Oprah's initial reaction was "No, no, I don't want to talk about that," because she wondered how on earth she could "make the story palatable to the woman who just got back from the soccer game and she's making dinner for her kids right now." She changed her mind the second the producer proposing the idea said, "I believe in my soul that this is the thing we should be doing." Oprah would *never* argue with a person's soul.

The Oprah Winfrey Show invited Dr. Catherine Hamlin to tell the story of her hospital in Ethiopia where, for the previous fifty years, she had treated more than twenty-four thousand young girls who suffered from fistula with a simple surgical procedure that restored their health and dignity. "We're giving a young, beautiful woman a new life," Dr. Hamlin explained. But she was nearly eighty, her hospital needed money to survive, and she was concerned she would not be around to raise the necessary funds in the future. After hearing her remarkable story, Oprah told Dr. Hamlin, "This is God's work on Earth," and immediately wrote a personal check, one that ending up paying for a new wing in the hospital. Similarly inspired, people in the

building—including Harpo employees and members of the audience—contributed money. Subsequently, Oprah visited Dr. Hamlin in Ethiopia to see her hospital and to meet some of the young girls who experienced life-altering miracles there every day.

In 2006, worldwide celebrity and activist Bono came to *The Oprah Winfrey Show* to raise awareness about the AIDS crisis in Africa, but he didn't do it in only a classic sit-down. Instead, he and Oprah left the studio and headed for Chicago's Michigan Avenue, where they shopped for special-edition (RED) products created specifically to raise money to combat AIDS. "I want the whole world to go (RED)!" Oprah said. Whenever shoppers purchased (RED)™ iPods, Converse sneakers, Gap T-shirts, Armani sunglasses and watches, and other participating items, a portion of profits from the sale of the branded products went to the Global Fund to help women and children affected by HIV/AIDS in Africa. The program demonstrated that the most ordinary activities, including shopping, could help someone in need.

Some of the world's most pressing problems, such as AIDS, famine, and war, were

Bono

She Moves in Mysterious Ways

About ten years ago, my friend and partner Bobby Shriver was talking to Oprah about getting me on her show to talk about the fight against extreme poverty. We thought: If we want to speak to America, speak to Oprah. We wanted to talk about the work we and a lot of other activists had been doing to get governments to cancel the debts the poorest countries on the planet owed to the wealthiest—a great way for the world to start the new millennium on the right foot. We had been twisting the arms of lawmakers, bank officials, and the people who run the IMF and the World Bank, and we had been having a lot of success.

Less so with Oprah. Her response was that she wasn't sure what we wanted from her audience. "How are you asking them to help?" she demanded. "And please don't tell me it's 'write your congressman,' because that's not enough. We need something concrete."

So I realized from the get-go two important things about Oprah's relationship with her audience. One, she stands guard over them—lioness energy, as Bobby called it. Two, she rejects all possibility of impotence. Oprah is no Grand Old Duke of York, leading her people to the top of the hill only to march them back down again.

The core of Oprah's message is simple: You are important. Not just to yourself, not just to her, but to the world. If you stand up and realize your potential, you will make an impact on the world, large or small. So it was not going to fly for me to come on her show, describe the fight against extreme poverty, and point to purely political rather than personal solutions. Thank you, try again.

It was less a rejection than a dare: Get your act together, boys. Improve your aim.

In 2002 she relented and let me past the gates, put me on the show. But there were conditions: For the activism to go down with an audience that was new to this issue, we had to talk about more than activism. More about me, in other words. Rarely am I averse to making things more about me, but here I actually had other things I wanted to talk about. So both of us were compromising.

On the show, we talked for a while, and then, right at the moment when I tried to enlist her audience in the campaign to get lifesaving AIDS drugs to Africa, where people would die without them, she took a seemingly un-Oprah-like stance and said what she knew was on the minds of the ten million people watching. She said, "A lot of them are women at home with their own children. What does this have to do with her life?" Especially when times were tough.

All that warmth you see Oprah emitting is real, every watt of it, but make no mistake: On her show, a free pass is not valid currency. She was putting me through my paces. I grasped for an answer. Eventually I said that you don't have to explain to a mother that a child's life—any child's life—has value. Maybe a man who sits in a boardroom might need an explanation, but a mother doesn't.

The whole place erupted. Her audience didn't need it explained, either. They knew. And of course, Oprah knew that they knew. As our activism progressed and we started the ONE campaign to fight extreme poverty, we could see that the moral compass of America was in the hands of women more than in men's, and that there was a very large heart beating in the heartland of America—in Chicago and the Midwest.

It was Oprah's voice ringing in our ears when we set up (RED) and gave her audience another good answer to the question of how they could help. (RED) gives them and all consumers a chance to change the world by how they shop. A (RED) product costs the same as a non-(RED) product, but a percentage of the profit on a (RED) iPod, Starbucks (RED) coffee, or a pair of (RED) Converse sneakers goes to save lives through the Global Fund to Fight AIDS, Tuberculosis, and Malaria.

The great brands have always had an emotional component. Think Apple, think Nike, think Starbucks, think Coca-Cola. (RED) is unabashedly a brand, and so is Oprah. And the big bang for us was when those two brands got together—when Oprah turned her whole show (RED). Something in my heart broke the moment I saw this girl in the audience, a girl from Missouri with a smile as wide as the Mississippi, wearing the Gap (RED) T-shirt with the word INSPI(RED) on the front. This T-shirt saves lives, she proclaimed. And as mad as that sounds, it's true, it saves lives. More of them now, thanks to that show.

If you want to speak to America, speak to Oprah. As I perhaps too often repeat, America is not just a country, it's an idea. An idea very much wrapped up in the concept of equality, justice, and freedom. These are revolutionary ideas—still hard to hold on to—especially equality. Some are still "more equal than others," and too many of us are judged by the way we look and by our economic or social status. It's a vertical world. We look up and down at people. Oprah's genius is that she looks across. And everyone who tunes in knows that.

You can't fake that. It's the way she sees the world, and it's the kind of influence she exerts on the world. And it explains everything we need to know about Oprah. It means she has no choice other than to respond when people are in trouble.

unfolding on the other side of the globe. But, as *The Oprah Winfrey Show* suggested, there were mounting humanitarian crises on the home front that required our immediate attention. Veteran journalist Tom Brokaw and First Lady Michelle Obama appeared on *Oprah* to discuss the plight of military families, in a show titled "The Bravest Families in America." The wars in Iraq and Afghanistan were the longest running in U.S. history, Brokaw said, yet less than 1 percent of the American population was bearing 100 percent of the battle. He thought it immoral that the men and women who were fighting on the front lines every day were not a part of our national consciousness. Instead of being rewarded when they came home, these brave soldiers, including those who were wounded in action, encountered apathy and neglect.

Corey Briest was hit by a bomb while serving in Iraq. He survived, but returned home blind and disabled, incapable of realizing his dream of becoming a paramedic. His children grew up in his hospital room as he endured physical therapy and attempted to recover from his severe brain injuries. His wife, Jenny, stood by him, trying to navigate what she called the "new normal" that was their arduous, day-to-day existence. But life was very difficult, and she was "angry for the people who walked away from us."

Brokaw urged Americans to demonstrate their concern and support for these underserved families. "Go to the door and say, how can I help?" he advised. Michelle Obama said she was so moved by these families that she wanted to be their voice. Military families were taught to be tough. They never ask for help, she pointed out.

Journalist Bob Woodward, who also appeared on the show, posed some provocative questions and answers: "What do we owe these people?" he asked. "Everything. What are we giving them? Not enough."

Another domestic crisis *The Oprah Winfrey Show* considered red-alert serious—and a target for sweeping social action—was the shocking deterioration of American schools. One of the most important people in Oprah's life was her fourth-grade teacher, Mrs. Mary Duncan, who instilled in her an undying

Top: Tom Brokaw, Sgt. Corey Briest, and his wife, Jenny Briest, January 27, 2011.

Bottom: Oprah is reunited with Mrs. Duncan, her favorite teacher, February 1, 1989.

Oprah takes on the crisis in American schools, pictured at right with Kevin Johnson, April 12, 2006.

respect for educators and the belief that education is transformative. "Education is freedom," said Oprah, "and that's how you make a huge difference in people's lives."

However, according to "American Schools in Crisis," an episode of *Oprah* that aired in 2006 (several years before the acclaimed documentary *Waiting for Superman* tackled the same subject), America's schools were in serious trouble. Oprah spoke to a number of experts about the meltdown. Guests Bill and Melinda Gates explained that a silent epidemic of failure threatened to doom generations of children to dead-end jobs and poverty. Lisa Ling investigated schools that were called "dropout factories." Anderson Cooper visited schools in Washington, D.C., that were literally falling down. America had lost its primacy. As videoed interviews showed, ill-taught Americans were hard put to name the first five presidents of the United States— Abraham Lincoln was a popular but incorrect choice—while students in China had no trouble answering the same question.

In addition to exposing problems, *The Oprah Winfrey Show* was committed to presenting stories about solutions and the people who made them possible. Star basketball player Kevin Johnson returned to his native Sacramento to found St. Hope Academy. He became principal and CEO of several schools in the area and worked with parents to prepare their children for college. He believed that poor education led to a higher crime rate and higher unemployment, while a better education led to more jobs, more opportunity, and a better community. Mike Feinberg and Dave Levin, the founders of KIPP Academy, taught their youngest students to aspire to college. And Bill and Melinda Gates spent over $1 billion creating new high schools throughout the country.

Oprah shined a light on altruists and social activists who tried to make a difference in the world, and encouraged others to follow their exemplary lead. "She believed that her role was that of a catalyst. She could use her show to tell stories of grassroots folks doing things in a tiny part of the world . . . going the extra mile, as a way to ignite in people a sense of caring, concern, and empathy," said former Harpo president Tim Bennett. Oprah wanted everyone to listen to the voice "inside of every human being that calls you to something greater than yourself." But mostly they listened to Oprah.

ChristmasKindness
South Africa 2002

For three weeks in December 2002, Oprah, members of her staff, and several of her friends traveled to South Africa to celebrate a Christmas they would remember for the rest of their lives. Oprah and her elves spent months picking out clothes, jeans, shoes, school supplies, toys, sporting goods, calculators, and solar radios, and something most African girls had never seen, black dolls, to hand-deliver to fifty thousand schoolchildren and orphans, many of whom had never received a present in their entire lives.

Their dream was to give children who had been hardest hit by the AIDS crisis (which was responsible for creating millions of orphans in South Africa and the rest of the world) a very special holiday. Oprah's favorite moment was when she got to say, "One, two, three. Open your presents!" The children were so happy that "the joy in the room was palpable. I had a joy headache. I felt it so deeply," Oprah said. She experienced a dramatic epiphany during the trip. "I realized in those moments why I was born, why I'm not married and do not have children of my own, because I knew that these are my children. . . . I made a decision to be a voice for those children, to empower them, to help educate them, so that the spirit that burns alive inside each of them does not die." She called it "one of the greatest experiences of my life," and her companions shared the feeling. There's a saying at Harpo: "If you want to make a staffer smile, ask about ChristmasKindness."

Top: Oprah stands with a crowd of children at the Phumza School in KwaZulu-Natal, December 22, 2003.

Bottom: Oprah gives a crown to a little girl at the Zanci School in Umtata, December 22, 2003.

Opposite: A child receives gifts and school supplies at God's Golden Acre in KwaZulu-Natal, December 22, 2003.

ChristmasKindness
South Africa 2002

Clockwise from top: Oprah helps a little girl put on her new shoes at God's Golden Acre in KwaZulu-Natal; Oprah gives toys to a child after leaving the Zimema School in KwaZulu-Natal; A little girl opens presents at God's Golden Acre in KwaZulu-Natal; Children leave Mshiywa School with their new backpacks, school supplies, shoes, clothes, and gifts, December 22, 2003.

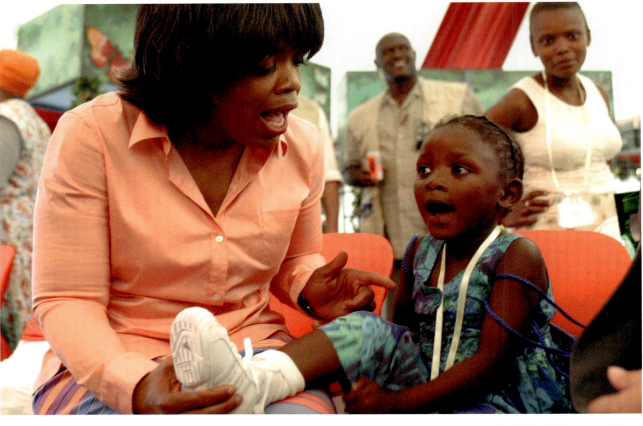

ChristmasKindness
South Africa 2002

Clockwise from top left:
Oprah tours Mshiywa
School in KwaZulu-Natal;
God's Golden Acre in
KwaZulu-Natal; Children
line up at the Zanci School
in Umtata to receive food,
clothing, shoes, school
supplies, books, and toys,
December 22, 2003.

Nelson Mandela

Oprah Winfrey

Oprah Winfrey's own story is an inspiration because she overcame almost every obstacle that a person might face. She is an icon to people all over the world because of her commitment to help those who have faced similar obstacles. We therefore salute a friend and a role model.

It is said over and over, but it is always true that young people are the future. Oprah shared our views that the gains of our democracy would be nullified if we did not properly educate our children and youth. She obviously recognized the potential in our youth. The Oprah Winfrey Leadership Academy for Girls—located near Johannesburg and educating girls in Grades 7 through 12—is therefore a wonderfully appropriate gift to the people of South Africa, one that will endure over many lifetimes.

When I went to the opening of her school, I looked at the shining faces of these young women and thought every one of them has the potential to be an Oprah Winfrey. The school is important because it will change the trajectory of these girls' lives and it will brighten the future of all women in South Africa.

Oprah understands that in Africa, women and girls have often been doubly disadvantaged. They have had the curse of low expectations and unequal opportunities. She is a model for all of them—and for all of us—of what one person can do to make a difference in the lives of others. That is why we consider her to be one of our heroes.

Soul Searching

"Faith is not something to grasp, it is a state to grow into."

–Mahatma Gandhi

"For me, there is no real power without spiritual power. A power that comes from the core of who you are and reflects all that you were meant to be."

The Oprah Winfrey Show's most ambitious—and most challenging—undertaking has been to awaken its audience to the power of the human spirit. "For me, there is no real power without spiritual power," Oprah Winfrey has said. "A power that comes from the core of who you are and reflects all that you were meant to be. A power that's connected to the source of things." Most people do not feel, or even understand, that connection because they have not learned to cultivate it. They know how to improve their bodies by eating sensibly and exercising several times a week, and how to expand their minds by doing crossword puzzles and learning new skills. But what is the process for improving something as intangible as the human spirit? The answer, according to Oprah, is the life-long pursuit of personal growth, and The Oprah Winfrey Show was committed to promoting growth from within.

Early on in her television career, Oprah embarked on a journey to enlightenment and she invited her audience to come along with her. Day after day on The Oprah Winfrey Show, ordinary people told extraordinary stories,

transforming viewers into dedicated students of humanity. They witnessed firsthand accounts of tragedy and triumph, weeping for victims and cheering for heroes. These encounters touched them emotionally and brought them a little closer to finding the passion, purpose, and principles they needed to build their own best lives. When learning vicariously wasn't enough, Oprah provided a carefully curated team of life coaches and spiritual advisors to help viewers chart their own paths to metaphysical fitness.

Oprah believed that life's challenging experiences presented the most meaningful opportunities for growth and self-discovery. "Every challenge can make you stronger if you allow it," she explained. A powerful Oprah episode that aired in 2004 illustrated her point with great poignancy. "I want everybody watching to think about this question," Oprah announced during the opening. "What was the worst day of your life? Well, perhaps your answer will be different after today's show," she suggested. For the next hour, mothers who were trying to come to terms with tragedies involving their children shared their horrific stories. Dr. Christine McFadden, a veterinarian in California, recalled the day she returned home from her daily walk to find that her four children had been brutally slain by her emotionally disturbed ex-husband, who also killed himself. She was joined by Cheli Porter, a mother who truly understood how Dr. McFadden felt because *her* vengeful ex-husband had murdered their three children.

Roni Bigelow's story was different, but no less disturbing. Always in a hurry, like most busy mothers, she left four of her five sons in the van for two minutes while she ran into her apartment to drop off the family parrot. When she returned, the van had exploded in flames, and her children, although still alive, were horribly burned.

Christy Robel relived the moment she dashed into a convenience store to buy her six-year-old a snack and watched in horror as a man who had been released from prison jumped behind the wheel of her car and drove away with her little boy in the back. Robel almost succeeded in pulling her son from the speeding car, but he became entangled in his seat belt and was dragged to his death before his mother's eyes.

In the tabloid world, these tragedies would be sensationalized illustrations of a dark, cruel universe, where innocent lives are destroyed by senseless twists of fate. But on *The Oprah Winfrey Show*, they became life lessons. As Oprah gently explored the bereaved mothers' emotions—their guilt, their sorrow, their anger, their uncertainty about the future—they benefited from talking openly about their innermost feelings and fears, and Oprah's audience learned from their heartfelt words. Dr. McFadden confessed that she frequently thought about ending her life. "I would have given anything just to go with my kids," she told Oprah matter-of-factly. But she kept postponing suicide because it was her mission to keep *their* memories alive. She had a profound effect on some viewers who had been contemplating suicide, but who changed their minds after hearing her story: If she could go on after such a terrible loss, so could they. Though Dr. McFadden genuinely believed that her life was over after her "worst day," she experienced a miraculous rebirth a few years later. She met a man,

fell in love, remarried, and eventually became the mother of twin daughters.

When Oprah asked Christy Robel how she found the strength to live after witnessing her son's death, her positive attitude was a panacea for her and a valuable lesson for others. Robel stressed that it was important to confront the pain that came with loss. Not only was it impossible to ignore because it waits in every corner, but she believed that grief was productive. "I feel like when you cry, when you're emotional, you're growing," she said. The same could be said of Oprah's viewers: When they responded emotionally to these deeply affecting stories, and they always did, they were growing, too.

In December 2004, design expert Nate Berkus, *The Oprah Winfrey Show*'s charismatic style guru, traveled with his partner, photographer Fernando Bengoechea, to a tropical paradise in Sri Lanka for a dream vacation. One morning, they noticed water trickling into their beachside hut, and suddenly they were engulfed by an enormous wave that propelled them into a raging cauldron of water and deadly debris. Their resort was directly in the path of the massive Indian Ocean tsunami. Miraculously, Berkus survived the first wave and surfaced to find Fernando swimming beside him. They desperately tried to hold on to each other when a second

Stage manager Dean Andersen, Cheli Porter, and Oprah hold up the quilt that Cheli's friends made to comfort her, April 23, 2004.

Mark Nepo

The Wisdom of an Open Heart

All the spiritual traditions encourage us to live in the open—no easy task given the suffering and injustice that fill every age. But heart-givers know that this openness releases our spiritual resilience. In my lifetime, I have seen the conversation around personal growth and spirit deepen and broaden from debating the credibility of spirit to the more useful exploration of how authentic personal growth leads us to a life of spirit and compassion for each other. For twenty-five years, *The Oprah Winfrey Show* has been a laboratory for spiritual discovery where authentic conversation has contributed to the evolution of our planet's collective soul.

When she received the Elie Wiesel Foundation's Humanitarian Award in May 2007, Oprah said, "Being a humanitarian is about using what you have to make someone else's life better." Oprah has spoken many times of her belief that spirituality is living with an open heart. Her life is a testament to the giving of one's heart to those before us and to all that is larger than us. There is a lineage of heart-givers committed to the manifestation of what Gandhi called "satyagraha." The word comes from Sanskrit (*satya* meaning "truth," *agraha* meaning "to grasp or hold"). Gandhi described satyagraha as "holding on to truth, hence truth-force." He also called it "love-force or soul-force." This commitment to holding on to the truth has made *The Oprah Winfrey Show* a steadfast commons where we can publicly explore the full range of our humanness with a commitment to how truth and kindness can reveal the wisdom of an open heart.

This is the work of personal growth in the realm of spirit: to face the prospect of dying without having truly lived, and the prospect of living without having truly loved. The rest are branches from these deep roots. And no one has ever been able to figure these out alone. Or enliven these alone. This is the journey before us all: to live well and love well, and to find each other. It is the finding of each other with truth and kindness that connects the individual soul's journey with the journey of community.

I have been personally moved by Oprah's presence on many levels. Since she was given *The Book of Awakening* for her birthday almost two years ago, we have become friends of spirit. What is inspiring to me is how her strength of self is such a sturdy container for the life-force of spirit to move through. Whether one-on-one or in front of thousands, her authenticity stays constant. Through this constancy of the authentic, the show has served as an educational ground for honest questions, open public dialogue, and the exploration of the intangible yet essential aspects of life. From hosting a town hall conversation in Williamson, West Virginia, in 1987 about the mayor's closing of the public pool because Michael Sisco, a gay man living with AIDS, went swimming there to convening two hundred men in 2010 who were sexually abused as children, Oprah's untiring effort to create a public space to educate ourselves in compassion has become her legacy.

This reminds me of another public learning ground in our time. It was Nelson Mandela who said, in the midst of his captivity on Robben Island, "We will make a university of our suffering." And in 1996, President Mandela created another experiment in satyagraha—in grasping or holding the truth—that our world is still trying to understand. He launched the Truth and Reconciliation Commission, in which those responsible for the atrocities of apartheid would publicly confess for the healing of their nation. And so, on April 15, 1996, the South African Broadcasting Corporation televised the first two hours of live hearings. The rest of the hearings were presented on television each Sunday from April 1996 to June 1998 in hour-long episodes.

I raise this because, in the words of Pumla Gobodo-Madikizela, a remarkable South African psychologist who worked for the commission and wrote the very compelling *A Human Being Died That Night*, this was and is the work of "making public spaces intimate." I raise this because this is the kind of education we're not given in school. I raise this because, in the lineage of heart-givers and truth-seekers, *The Oprah Winfrey Show* has been making public spaces intimate for us to explore the kinship of all things and how truth and kindness, through listening and holding, are the eternal initiations into making that kinship known.

I believe and give my heart to the notion that spirituality is listening for and living into the soul's place on Earth. A life of spirit, regardless of what path you choose, begins with a person's acceptance that they are part of something larger than themselves. And the want to know who we really are and to know the truth of our existence and our connection is, to me, the fundamental life-giving question that the heart commits to, once opened by love or suffering.

In receiving the humanitarian award that night in May 2007, Oprah also said, "We are all free agents for the Divine. We are managers of the spiritual forces within us that can, if we choose, have the power to transform our lives and the lives of the people we know." I think we are all hungry to be transformed by this unending connection that waits like air and light between us.

This transformation of love-force and truth-force that makes public spaces intimate appears in the best of times and the worst of times. In his brave, sensitive, and unflinching memoir, *Night*, Elie Wiesel recalls the death march he and thousands were forced to make in the ice and snow of an Eastern European night, forced to run barefoot for hours toward Buchenwald. In anticipation of the Allied forces, the SS butted and pistol-whipped the emaciated prisoners on and on. If anyone slowed or stopped, they were trampled. If someone fell, they were shot. In the midst of this inexplicable hell, a poor soul near Wiesel stumbled to the ground and others fell on top of him. There was so much going on that the guards just beat them all to their feet.

Of all the harrowing, poignant, and unspeakable things Elie Wiesel witnessed as a fifteen-year-old, this small anonymous moment of love-force and truth-force is what has stayed with me. I imagine it at the oddest times—while driving home in the rain, while walking the dog in the snow. It won't let go of me. I think because it holds the essence of community. For this moment is a testament to the lengths we'll go to care for each other if led or pushed to our true nature.

How we are led and pushed to our true nature is what spirituality and personal growth are all about. This is at the center of the public effort known as *The Oprah Winfrey Show*. I wrote Oprah months ago that I was feeling the pull of the world and asked how she meets this pull. She wrote back, "The only thing that makes sense is to meet each moment with the truth of who you are. I'll help you in any way I can." The truth and kindness rising here is at the core of the deepest education. Like heart-givers before her, Oprah Winfrey is a soul-force who leads us through the salt of truth till the honey of kindness awakens our true nature.

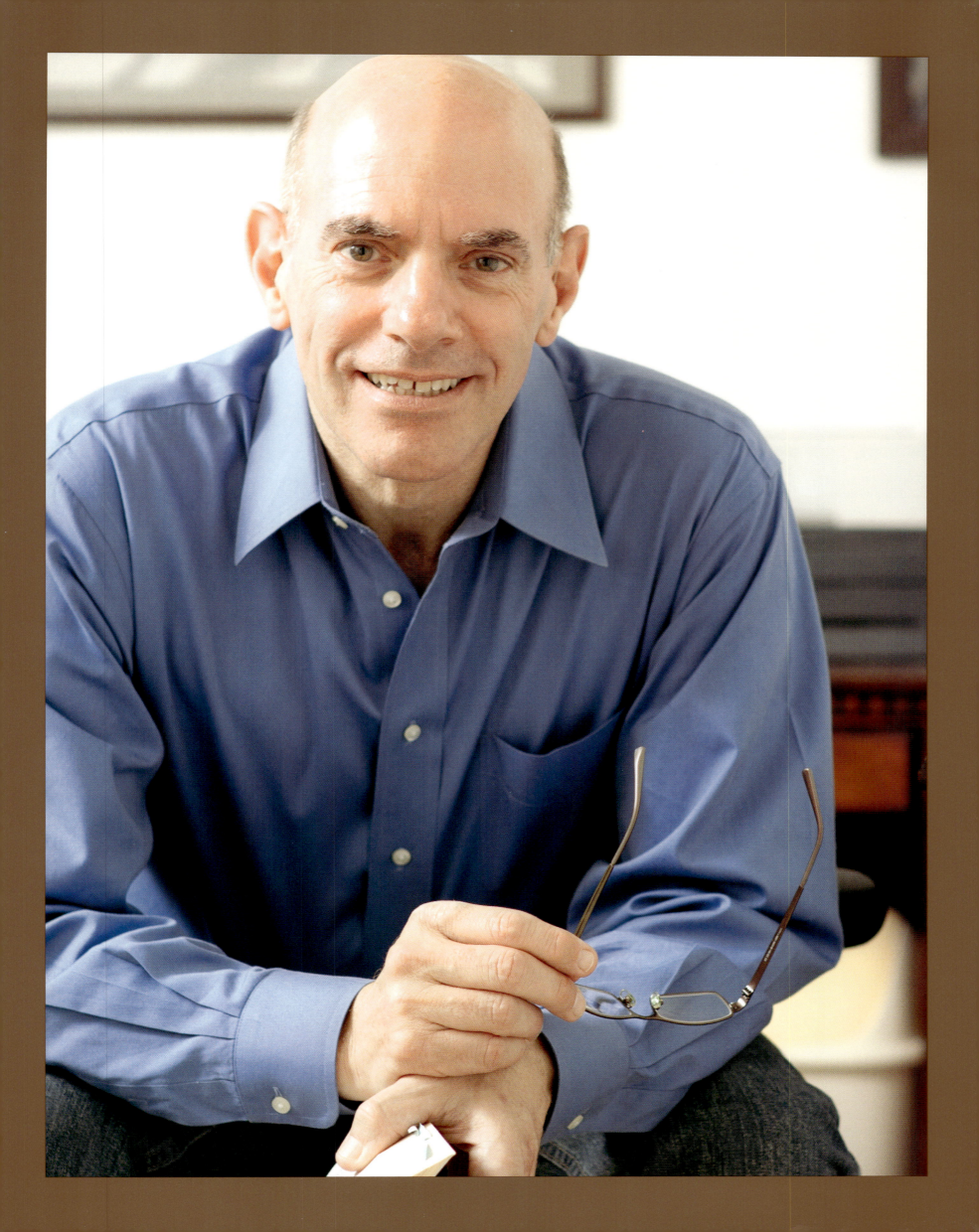

Nate Berkus recounts the devastating events of the South Asia tsunami, which claimed the life of his partner, Fernando Bengoechea, January 17, 2005.

wave tore them apart. Berkus finally made his way to safety on a hilltop, but Fernando was lost. Eventually, he was presumed dead.

Three weeks later, Berkus appeared on *The Oprah Winfrey Show* to discuss his terrifying experience. He was sad and vulnerable when he spoke of Fernando, but instead of focusing on his personal loss, he reached deep inside himself to find the strength to talk about the incredible bravery, kindness, and generosity he witnessed during the disaster. Berkus believed that the tragedy, as terrible as it was, brought out the best in people. After spending two days without proper clothing or shoes, he remembered being moved to tears when a concerned doctor gave him a clean shirt and a pair of flip-flops. "Despite the death and the destruction and the horror, there was an incredible amount of beauty going on at that time," he emphasized. "The kindness that was shown, not only to me, but to one another . . . you could *feel* the humanity."

The kindness continued when Berkus returned home to Chicago. Oprah thanked the thousands of people who sent him "the most beautiful letters we've ever received at our show." A woman named Kym wrote, "Dear Nate, millions of people care about you. We can see your sweet spirit even though we have only watched you on TV. Maybe you will be able to feel the love coming from all of us. I hope so." Another concerned fan said that when she first heard the news she "gasped like it was someone in my own family. You put a personal face on this for so many of us who regularly watch you on OPRAH." Berkus read every single letter

and credited the overwhelming outpouring of love and compassion with lifting him out of despair and pointing him toward recovery.

At the end of the show, Oprah announced that the Angel Network would fund a million-dollar recovery program in Sri Lanka. In a wonderfully humanitarian triangulation, people who cared about Nate Berkus extended their concern to the tsunami victims on the other side of the world, creating a giant web of empathy. "The yearning to help strangers across the globe, that is truly, I believe, more powerful than any tsunami," Oprah told her audience. "Together, if we choose to be, we all can be the ultimate force of nature." Even a tragedy of epic proportions could have a positive outcome when people committed to helping each other.

Jacqui Saburido, another unforgettable survivor who appeared on *The Oprah Winfrey Show*, showed viewers the true meaning of forgiveness, which Oprah now defines as "giving up the hope that the past could have been any different." In 1999, Saburido was a beautiful, young Venezuelan woman who loved to sing, dance, and live life to the full-est. She moved to Texas to study English and, one September night, attended a birth-day party with her new friends. On the way home, their car was struck by a drunk driver and some of the passengers perished in the crash. Saburido was trapped inside the car when it burst into flames and was burned beyond recognition. After having been in a coma for ten months, she awoke to pain, dis-figurement, endless surgeries, and the shock-ing realization that her life would never, ever, be what she imagined. "I miss my body. I miss my independence. I miss my opportunities, my future, because it won't be the same," she told Oprah. "Sometimes my soul wants to get out. I want to be in another body, you know, that I can do whatever I want to do, but I don't know how."

Nonetheless, Saburido managed to carry on. Yes, she affirmed during the interview, she was happy that she survived. "I want to live a lot of things that I haven't enough time to do," she said. As difficult as her life was, she did not succumb to regret or despair. In fact, she allowed herself only five minutes a day to feel sorry for herself. And she refused to hate Reggie Stephey, the young man who was responsible for the crash, because she believed "Forgiveness is important for the soul, for my own soul, you know, to live in peace." Stephey, who served seven years in

prison for manslaughter, called Saburido's pardon "life-changing." With her forgiveness, *he* could go on.

A horrific incident that could have left Saburido bitter and Stephey destroyed became a catalyst for life-affirming behavior. Saburido courageously made a public service announcement, using her tragedy as a condemnation of drunk driving. Stephey's mother, who appeared on *The Oprah Winfrey Show* alongside Saburido and was awed by her kind, generous spirit, delivered her own cautionary message to the audience that day. She urged parents not to be rigid with their children: Had she been less judgmental, her son might have felt more comfortable calling her for a ride that night, and tragedy could have been averted.

Nate Berkus was a model of compassion, Jacqui Saburido the embodiment of forgiveness, and Monica Jorge, whom Oprah described as a "Warrior Mom," was a dynamo of pure purpose. Immediately after she gave birth to her second child in 2007, Jorge's body was attacked by a fatal strain of flesh-eating bacteria, and the only cure was amputation. She lost her arms and legs, but instead of giving up on life, which she had every right to do, Jorge bounced back immediately and headed home to take care of her family. "You make do with what you have," she told Oprah when she appeared on the show in 2008. Life wasn't easy, but Jorge knew what was truly important: With or without limbs, "I could still love my girls," she said contentedly.

The courageous individuals who shared their stories on *The Oprah Winfrey Show* sometimes did so at great personal cost. It was difficult for Kathy Bray, whose ten-year-old son Scott was accidentally killed by a friend who was playing with his father's handgun, to appear on the show only three weeks after the incident. But she wanted to warn other parents about the danger of keeping a gun in the house. Todd Costello, a grieving father, talked to Oprah about the day he mistakenly left his infant son in the car instead of dropping him off at day care. Baby Tyler died because his father was preoccupied with thoughts about work when he closed the windows and walked away from the car. Costello has not been able to forgive himself,

Top: Jean Stephey hugs Jacqui Saburido, the woman her son tragically injured in a drunk-driving incident, November 25, 2003.

Bottom: Jenny McCarthy and Monica Jorge, September 24, 2008.

While his "Phil-isms" made everyone (especially Oprah) laugh, there was no mistaking the powerful truth behind Dr. Phil's folksy words.

but he talks about his experience, hoping to prevent other parents from making the same fatal mistake.

These stories, and stories like them, served as the core curriculum for "Humanity 101" on *The Oprah Winfrey Show*. But for those who needed a more direct, turbo-charged approach to personal growth, there was straight-talking Dr. Phil McGraw. With his signature blend of humor, insight, candor, and practicality, Dr. Phil could meet any problem head-on and quickly whip up a meaningful resolution, Texas-style.

While his "Phil-isms" made everyone (especially Oprah) laugh, there was no mistaking the powerful truth behind Dr. Phil's folksy words. He told a self-absorbed bride-to-be that she was preparing for the wedding, but not for the marriage. Speaking on behalf of a young husband whose wife was selfishly driving their family into bankruptcy, he told her, "I will drop you like a bad habit before I will let those kids fall by the wayside, okay?" He told an insensitive husband not to "dog-pile" his wife "in the foyer" (a comment that amused, but mystified Oprah), and he insisted to some family members engaged in a feud that no matter "how flat you make a pancake, it's got two sides." He had a gift for using simple, colorful language to help troubled people understand their problems and take the necessary steps to fix them.

Comic colloquialisms aside, one of Dr. Phil's greatest moments on *The Oprah Winfrey Show* was a very serious encounter with Jo Ann Compton, a bereaved mother who had lost her will to live. Her eighteen-year-old daughter was murdered in 1988 but, a decade later, Compton was still fixated on her death and extremely depressed. Dr. Phil pointed out that her daughter would never have wanted her mother to be so unhappy for so many years, and that it was a betrayal for Compton to focus on the day of her death when she should be "celebrating the event of her life."

Clockwise from top: Dr. Phil McGraw and Oprah, April 23, 2002; Dr. Martha Beck on how to "Stop Being a Doormat," June 13, 2002; Carla gets sound advice about her spending habits from Dr. Phil while her husband, Brent, looks on, March 6, 2001.

Both Dr. Phil and Oprah saw a look of surprise—and then comprehension—on Compton's face as she admitted, "I never thought of it that way." It was a classic "aha" moment, which Oprah liked to say was "remembering what you already know." Before the show, Compton had made up her mind to commit suicide, but Dr. Phil's words changed everything: Once she *felt* more positive, her life actually became more positive.

There were several less colorful (who could be as colorful as Dr. Phil?), but equally effective, game-changing coaches and therapists who appeared regularly on the show: Dr. Martha Beck, who encouraged women to stand up to life and "Stop Being a Doormat," and Cheryl Richardson, who devised concrete ways for women to say "no" and beat the "disease to please" syndrome. Richardson suggested a series of exercises to accomplish that goal, including: "For one week,

keep track of the times you say 'yes' when you don't want to," and "If you could say 'no' to someone without consequences, who would it be?" The idea was to reclaim personal time without feeling guilty, and to take small, deliberate steps toward a more purposeful life.

Psychotherapist and ordained rabbi M. Gary Neuman came to *The Oprah Winfrey Show* on a special mission to heal two children with wounded spirits. Eleven-year-old Daisy and seven-year-old Kris were devastated because their mother left home, and they somehow feared that her departure—and their parents' divorce—was *their* fault. Even a well-intentioned parent could be oblivious to the signs of a child's suffering during times of emotional upheaval. Kris cried for his mother on camera, breaking hearts all over the country, while Daisy was equally touching when she pretended to

Oprah comforts Kris while he and his sister, Daisy, reveal the pain of their parents' divorce to their father, Jim, September 26, 2007.

Marianne Williamson

Living Her Best Life

I'm one of quite a few authors who have been fortunate enough to have their books showcased on the *The Oprah Winfrey Show*. In the years since Oprah enthused about my first book, *A Return to Love*, on her program in 1992, I've had countless people say to me, "I first saw you on *Oprah*." For those of us who've poured our hearts and souls into what we've written and then had our books discussed on her program, Oprah's support has meant millions of people reading our words who otherwise might never have been exposed to them. On the subject of spirituality, Oprah addressed the topics of love, forgiveness, finding the true self, service, and compassion—eternal ideas to be sure, but heretofore hardly the topic of mainstream American conversation (believe it or not)—and did more than any other single individual to turn them into popular mantras that blare throughout our contemporary culture. Such is her power, and such is her heart.

The convergence of spirituality and *The Oprah Winfrey Show* has less to do with the spiritual authors she has showcased and more to do with the way she herself has chosen to lead her life and use her program as a force for good. Everything we do is infused with the consciousness with which we do it, and it's been Oprah's willingness to expose her own heart—her wishes, her struggles, her pain—that has given her show such spiritual force. She wasn't just delivering a message to her audience; she was trying to accept it for herself first. When she talked about a subject, read a book, or interviewed its author, her enthusiasm carried the force of her own conviction and sincerity. When it comes to spirituality and her celebration of its power, the message was "Watch out, world." And watch, we did.

The show itself became a vehicle of love in millions of people's lives. It's one thing to talk about love; it's another thing to work with the FBI by finding child predators and helping to bring them to justice, exposing the prevalence of domestic violence, or illuminating injustices toward women and children around the world. It's one thing to hold up a book saying that the love and light within us is the essence of who we are; it's another thing to dedicate your entire program to Living Your Best Life and giving viewers exposure to the experts and best practices that could help them do that.

Despite the dogmatic insistence by some that only organized religion has the right to expound on spiritual subjects, Oprah risked the ire of those who were not enthusiasts, stood her ground, and continued to explore the vicissitudes of spiritual understanding. Her Live Your Best Life slogan was the perfect nondenominational and popular motto for a serious spiritual message: that finding the Light within, the Christ within, the Buddha within, the Shechinah within, or any other eternal truth within is the purpose of our lives. Leave it to Oprah to take what is the most profound concept in the world and turn it into an easily understandable, practical path for living. She didn't exactly wave a wand, but then, on some invisible level, it's as though she did. There will never be a perfect accounting of how many hearts and minds were opened, how many depressed people found hope, or how many tears turned into laughter because of something someone saw on *Oprah*. No mere television show could do this; only the spiritual force of a noble personality could bring that much light into so many people's homes.

I was once strolling with Oprah through her beautiful property at her home in California. After walking silently for a few minutes, I turned to her and said, "Why you?" And she answered me with a touching humility and honesty. "I don't know."

I have watched her long enough, however, that I think I do know. Having observed her both professionally and personally for years, I've seen a couple of things that are spiritual keys to her enormous success.

The first is generosity. Whenever anything good comes into her life, Oprah's first thought—and I do mean first—is how to give it away to everyone else. She likes an idea? "I have to tell everybody." Something is helpful? "People need to know about this!" If she hears an exciting idea, she wants to tell everyone else about it as quickly as possible. If she reads a good book, she wants everyone to know about it immediately. It's as if there's no fraction of hesitation between the goodness that comes to her and the goodness she gives out. Whether she was presenting an idea to people to help them open their minds or giving a house to a family of modest means so they could have a place to raise their children, the entire world has witnessed Oprah's generosity of spirit. She's generous not just because she's so prosperous; I'm convinced that she's prosperous because she's so generous.

The second is compassion. As Oprah has said on her program, "Everyone just wants to be heard." No one who has ever watched Oprah conduct an interview has doubted her ability or willingness to listen deeply to another person express their pain. And she extends this talent not only to her guest, but also to members of her audience. And it wasn't just the compassion shown in front of the cameras that gave *The Oprah Winfrey Show* such spiritual force. From the Leadership Academy for Girls in South Africa to countless other projects that helped uplift people in America and around the world, the show has been a constant generator of compassion-in-action.

Through her television show, Oprah has promulgated simple spiritual truths that change people's lives—that love is the answer; that we are both empowered by and answerable to a Higher Power; that forgiveness matters; that there is always hope; that truth sets us free; that we must take responsibility for our lives; that integrity counts; that people should be held accountable; that we mustn't tolerate evil; that we must care for one another; that we must protect our children; that one person can make a difference; that we can and should make amends when we know we've been wrong—these are the spiritual principles *The Oprah Winfrey Show* has etched into the minds of millions of its viewers. The power that turned all that into a genuine force that literally changed the landscape of our modern society was the fact that Oprah herself—not always easily, but as honestly and authentically as she could—was trying to live that way herself. Her power lay not in whether she always found the miracle she was seeking but in the fact that there was absolutely no doubt that she was trying her best and being honest with all of us about her search.

While *The Oprah Winfrey Show* has come to its natural end, its effect will live on in the way it has touched the hearts and opened the minds of so many. Television will never quite be the same, and Oprah's viewers will never quite be the same, either. Millions of us will think more uplifted thoughts, we will struggle to be our best selves, we will read serious books, we will raise our children more consciously, and we will be warmed by knowing that one person—a woman who, while she might not have known us personally, knew us better in some way than almost anyone else because she knew our deepest yearnings and she spoke to them. In some mysterious way, it's as though she heard us all. And she passionately cared.

be strong. Neuman reminded parents to speak honestly to their children about divorce because what they imagine is probably much worse than the reality. On the other hand, parents should avoid being openly critical of a former spouse. "When you criticize the other parent, you criticize your child's DNA," he cautioned. Dr. Phil also believed that arguing was destructive. "When you argue in front of your children you change them," he said—sound advice that was simple and direct.

Sometimes, "finding your way" was a more complicated process that required deeper resources. *The Oprah Winfrey Show* recognized the importance of cultivating the spirit, and introduced viewers to advisors, or thinkers, who could awaken them to their inner selves and help them realize their potential. "Anybody who knows me," said Oprah, "will tell you nothing makes me happier than talking about this, because spirituality, to me, is the greatest discovery of life . . . to recognize that you are more than your body and more than your mind." However, she was careful to distinguish between spirituality and religion. "You can be spiritual regardless of your religious beliefs," she explained. "Spirituality is that yearning for something more . . . something higher." She also made the point that, far from being "ooh-ooh, whoo-oo" or way out, spirituality is "the most grounding awakening path you can ever pursue in your life."

"Spiritual teachers show up in many different sizes, shapes, races, and ages on this show," Oprah told her audience.

"Spiritual teachers show up in many different sizes, shapes, races, and ages on this show," Oprah told her audience during an episode dedicated to "Finding Your Spiritual Path." Marianne Williamson was one of the first "teachers" on the show, and Oprah thanked her for the life-affirming prayer that sets her on course every morning: "that this time on the planet be spent to reach the highest level of humanity that is possible for each one of us." Anyone, regardless of religious orientation, could aspire to that goal.

Gary Zukav, author of *The Seat of the Soul*, connected spirituality to intuition and intention when he appeared on *The Oprah Winfrey Show*. He believed that intuition—almost a sixth sense—enables a person to follow his heart,

I not only want to fulfill the mission of my purpose this trip to the Planet Earth, I want to do it consciously so that I can revel in its splendor.

I really have learned I think how everything happens for a reason, and I am conscious of trying to look for the reason instead of the incident itself. But as I grow I wish to grow to understand the Oneness and to be able to teach it and share it.

Right now I'm wrestling with the notion of how, when, release to teach it under a structured setting. Stedman says just do it and you'll

learn how to do it. Expand it and so forth as you go forward— teach 3 or 4. lessons,

Too many people wait for things to be ideal before trying like Julius waiting to get thin before going home.

Me waiting to get thin before living my life.

I'm ready to move forward and even in the past couple months I can see myself headed in that direction. I've maintained 2 weeks now of consistent exercise if I won't ne... today. That's progress. I still haven't worked on the food, even with Rosie, still consuming too much— but I'm getting there

Pages from one of Oprah's personal journals, August 23, 1994.

while intention, which Zukav described as "the single most powerful energy in our lives," is the fuel that runs the soul. Use your *intuition* to set a moral compass, he advocated, and move with *intention* as you follow its course.

Elizabeth Lesser, another revered spiritual teacher and the author of *Broken Open*, used the analogy of the tightly wound bud to illustrate the journey to spiritual awareness. In order for a bud to blossom, it has to break open. It is during difficult broken times—an illness, the loss of a child, a marriage, or a job—that growth occurs: "When we open into our brokenness, that's when we blossom," Lesser noted. Oprah concurred: "I think that when you have the most devastating things happen to you, that those are your holiest moments. That's where you get to see who you really are."

Admittedly, it can be difficult, even counter-intuitive, to find the "good" in "bad." Sarah Ban Breathnach, author of *Simple Abundance*, told Oprah that it is human nature to focus on what is wrong and lacking in life. However, she offered a tool designed to transform negative emotions into positive ones: a gratitude journal. Quoting the poet John Milton, who said, "Good, the more communicated, grows," Breathnach recommended keeping a daily list of everything that makes you thankful in

your life. Oprah laughingly recalled that when she started her gratitude journal, she was usually grateful for food things—she'd write "sorbet" or "Loved that bread I had with the soup" on her list. With practice, she became more contemplative, and when she started to appreciate what she had, she began to see that she had more.

Perhaps the youngest "teacher" to appear on *The Oprah Winfrey Show*—and certainly the one with the oldest soul—was eleven-year-old Mattie Stepanek. Mattie was born with a rare form of muscular dystrophy that had claimed the lives of his three siblings before they reached the age of four. Although he had to endure life in a wheelchair, breathing tubes, and operations, Mattie managed to survive the disease and, more importantly, to transcend it. No amount of pain or adversity could dim his unique spirit. "I've always had three wishes," said young Mattie. "One, to have my books published so I can spread my message of peace through the world; two, to talk peace with my hero, Jimmy Carter; and to meet with Oprah Winfrey."

All of his wishes came true. Mattie published poetry he had been writing since he was three; he spoke to Jimmy Carter, who became his staunchest admirer; and he met Oprah, with whom he developed a very special

Tererai Trent

Oprah also found inspiration in the life of **Tererai Trent**, who was the subject of a show called "You'll Never Give Up on a Dream After Seeing This Woman." Trent was born in a poor village in Zimbabwe, denied an education, and married off to an abusive husband at the age of eleven. Yet she dreamed of moving to America to achieve the impossible: a bachelor's degree, a master's, *and* a doctorate. Somehow, Trent managed to turn each one of those impossible dreams into a proud reality, giving new meaning to the term "personal growth."

In Season 25, Oprah invited Tererai Trent back to the show, announcing that she was her all-time favorite guest because she represented "everything this show has stood for and tried to say for twenty-five years. She absolutely embodies every story, every moment of perseverance, believing, gratitude, you name it." Oprah also said that she was honoring Trent's remarkable journey by donating $1.5 million to rebuild the primary school in Trent's village with the help of Save the Children.

Clockwise from top:
Tererai visits the site where she had buried the small box that contained a list of her dreams, October 1, 2009; Jo Luck of Heifer International visited Tererai Trent's village in Zimbabwe in 1991 and inspired Tererai to write down her dreams, which she insisted could become a reality, October 1, 2009; Oprah names Tererai Trent her all-time favorite guest and donates $1.5 million to help her rebuild a school in Zimbabwe, May 20, 2011.

Clockwise from top left:
Tom Shadyac and Oprah,
April 20, 2011; Oprah hosting
A New Earth webinar, April
9, 2008; Sarah Ferguson,
the Duchess of York,
May 11, 2011.

relationship. She called him "my guy," and said, "I could not believe so much wisdom, so much power, so much grace, so much strength, and love could come from one little boy." Whenever Mattie visited the show, he impressed everyone with his unshakable faith and optimism. "I want people to know my life philosophy," he told her, "to play after every storm." In his life, there were storms every day.

Sometimes, the most unlikely people, including an English duchess and a Hollywood director, offered important insights about personal growth on *The Oprah Winfrey Show*. High-spirited Sarah Ferguson, better known as "Fergie," seemed to be the Royal-next-door when she married Prince Andrew in 1986 and became England's Duchess of York. But their divorce in 1996 marked the beginning of her downward slide, culminating in a bribery scandal that exposed her financial and emotional desperation. The Sarah Ferguson who appeared on *Oprah* in 2011 wanted to reclaim her life and understood that she had to own her mistakes. "I will accept everything I've done, and I will now just go forward. I must go forward," she told Oprah. "I remember one wonderful lady in Sierra Leone who said to me, 'They can take your country, but they can't take your soul.' And I feel that I can come back from this. It will take a long time, but I think I'm authentically myself sitting here right now, and I'm going to give it a good shot."

Tom Shadyac was best known for directing blockbuster films such as *Ace Ventura,*

The Nutty Professor, and *Bruce Almighty.* He embraced the lavish millionaire lifestyle that came with his success, until he realized that true happiness comes from a simpler, more authentic life of compassion and connection. He downsized his "stuff," moved into a mobile home, and made *I Am,* a provocative and inspirational documentary that poses the eye-opening questions: What's wrong with our world, and what can we do to make it better? Oprah appreciated Shadyac's observations and called the show "exhilarating." "For me, a show's only great if there's an 'aha' moment when you think, 'I get that, I know that,'" she explained. "That happened at least four or five times during today's show."

Matters pertaining to the soul were not typical topics for a television talk show, especially one that was so entertaining. But, *The Oprah Winfrey Show* considered spirituality, or personal growth, to be as important as physical, psychological, or emotional well-being. Eventually, Oprah's audience felt exactly the same way. In 2008, she introduced her viewers to Eckhart Tolle's revolutionary book, *A New Earth,* which urged people to live in the "now," to think positively, and to "be the change" that could transform the world. When Oprah cohosted with Tolle a ten-part webinar exploring his philosophy, millions of viewers considered the classes a mandatory learning experience, a sign that, thanks to the influence of *The Oprah Winfrey Show*, they *were* growing, and in ways they never imagined.

Dr. Phil McGraw

All That Is Oprah

When I reflect on how *The Oprah Winfrey Show* has touched people's lives, it becomes a very personal reflection. Although I must admit that when I first met Oprah in 1997, I had never once watched one of her shows from start to finish. Of course, I knew who she was. You can't live on planet Earth and not know that Oprah is one of the most famous and powerful women in America. But in all honesty, I wasn't sure what exactly she did that made her such a beloved figure to so many millions of people. I just didn't watch daytime television because, like a lot of folks, I worked during the day. I had a PhD in psychology and was president of a national litigation-consulting firm in Dallas. Our team of professionals worked with lawyers to create trial strategies, jury profiles, and jury selections; conducted mock trials; helped to prepare witnesses to testify effectively; and constructed graphics and visuals for trial. We were a soup-to-nuts trial-support team, pretty much a Toys"R"Us for lawyers.

That, in fact, was the reason I was asked to fly to Chicago to meet Oprah. My firm had been retained to help with her defense in what would come to be known as the "Mad Cow" case. A group of West Texas cowmen had alleged that one of her shows about the dangers of mad cow disease had damaged the beef industry. I assumed it would be a routine procedure where I would work with Oprah on her upcoming testimony, design and run a few mock trials, work with the lawyers on developing trial strategy, help to select the jury, and then move on to the next case. What I didn't know was that I was about to meet a woman who not only would become one of my dearest friends, but who would also turn out to be one of the most powerfully pivotal people in my life. She would change the course of my life and that of my family in ways I could never have imagined.

And so it began. I worked closely with Oprah for the next two-plus years. A small group of us actually lived together for weeks, 24/7, in a bed-and-breakfast in Amarillo, Texas, where the trial took place. Oprah and I spent many, many hours there just talking—talking about the things that mattered in our lives, about struggles and disappointments, and about our joys and accomplishments. We talked about how to create, embrace, and live a truly authentic life—a life driven from the inside out—and we talked about the power of being able to claim one's dreams in the real world. When you live with someone day in and day out—especially at a time when you feel as if you are behind enemy lines—you come to know them in a very deep and real way. My dad used to call those types of relationships "foxhole buddies." Given some insomnia in a "foreign land," the two of us would meet in the kitchen in the middle of the night and sit around the kitchen table eating pie and talking. Sometimes for hours, often with two forks, eating right out of the pan! I mean, let's not stand on etiquette when it comes to pie!

We won that case, and it was really a victory for America, a victory for free speech. The day the verdict came in, she invited her entire legal team to be on her show. When it was my turn to be introduced, she became quite emotional and said, "Phil gave myself back to me." To say the least, I was deeply moved. What I wanted to tell the audience was: "Not true! The 'giver' here is Oprah, not me." I wanted to say that during our weeks together, Oprah was not only one of the most mesmerizing people I had ever met, she was one of the most giving. She always had time to regard me as a person and friend first, not just as a hired professional. She took the time and put forth the effort to meet and form relationships with my wife and children—relationships, by the way, that have lasted to this very day. I wanted to tell the audience that just by being in the same room with Oprah, I genuinely felt better about who I was. I wanted to tell them about that moment, after one excruciating day in the courtroom in which lawyers from the other side ripped into her, she said to me, "You know, there is a difference between thinking you deserve to be happy and knowing you are worthy of happiness." This was a woman who never stopped talking about the importance of being "real" and keeping priorities in order, no matter the circumstances. She always seemed to know exactly who she was.

Needless to say, I became a huge fan and a regular viewer of her show, watching in rapt fascination as she gently persuaded her guests to open up about such previously taboo issues as sexual abuse, incest, addiction, depression, domestic abuse, sexuality, and AIDS. Her show was a source of comfort and inspiration, as well as a place that pushed all of us to think in ways many of us had never thought before. Along the way, she helped her audience understand who exactly they were—and, just as important, who they could be. It was not unusual that after an *Oprah* show, people were able to talk, some of them for the first very time, about what their lives were really all about.

Then came the day when her producer called and said Oprah wanted me to come on the show as an expert. I was more than a little surprised and a little confused. Oprah knew I wasn't one of those guys who walked down the road less traveled, sipped chicken soup for the soul, journeyed toward the light, or sought my inner child. She also knew her staff didn't think I was, to put it mildly, much of a fit for television.

And why should they? I mean, come on, I was big, bald, and blunt. I often used cornpone sayings I had learned growing up in the South. I also wasn't much for mincing words. I tell people the truth as I see it no matter if it's what they want to hear or not. But Oprah insisted that the time was right for her audience to get some commonsense, straightforward advice. She said she wanted me to tell her guests and viewers "how it is" just like I had done with her. She wanted people to have someone in their lives who would tell them what they needed to hear instead of patting their hands and placating them. So—who am I to argue with Oprah Winfrey? I said, "Okay, I'll give it a shot."

Before long, I was spending every Tuesday beside her on the stage, talking to her guests about critical issues, and not once did she suggest I back off or go easy. I had never felt so vital and relevant in making a difference. What's most amazing, she got as real as her guests did about her own life. I remember when I said to a guest something along the lines of "We don't use food, we abuse food. It's not what you eat, but why you eat that has you in the problem that you're in." Oprah cheerfully responded, "Well, there are some people who are just genetically disposed to being smaller." I looked at her and said, "But the fact is, that ain't you, is it, Oprah?" She could have yelled, "Give him the HOOK!" But she just threw back her head and roared with laughter. That is Oprah.

And then one day she said, "Okay, Phil, people need to hear you every day. It's time for you to go off and do your own show." It was an amazing act of generosity—and of love. But again, that's Oprah. Every day of her life, she has been driven to pass on the message that it doesn't matter where you come from, it doesn't matter what did or did not happen in your childhood, and it doesn't matter what place you find yourself in right now. You still have the power to make real changes and real choices to manifest your dreams. It's never too late to seize that moment when you can make all things right.

I have been asked more times than I can count, "Is Oprah really as nice as she seems? Is she really how she's portrayed on TV?" I always respond the same way: "No, she is nicer than she is portrayed. Television is not a big-enough medium to capture all that is Oprah Winfrey." Outside of my family, there are few people in this world who are more important to me than Oprah. It's not because she gave me a new career when I was fifty years old. I was already blessed with success and very happy with what I was doing. It's because she is so remarkably empathetic, so caring, and so wise—that rare person who honors the life and experience of everyone she comes across. Oprah is, and always will be, a clarion voice for all that is good. Personally, I can't wait for her next chapter!

Mattie Stepanek

Mattie Stepanek's smile was wondrous to see. In many ways, it was a classic little-boy grin—wide, gap-toothed, and sunny, redolent of the "snips and snails and puppy-dog tails" of the old nursery rhyme, an expression of the joy within. Smiling came surprisingly easy to this child who regarded life from a wheelchair, a respirator at his side. Mattie never allowed his physical handicaps, or the knowledge that his young life could be cut short at any time by his rare form of muscular dystrophy, to get in the way of his dreams.

Mattie envisioned a better world and shared his message of love and peace through his poetry and art. He wrote seven books of poems and created vibrant paintings that reflected the hope and optimism that infused his life every day. He gave new meaning to the term "wise beyond his years," because wisdom seemed to come naturally to him. When he heard that his friend Oprah was contemplating ending her show on its twentieth anniversary, he sent her a long email listing the reasons why she should carry on until Season 25. His logic was indisputable. Unlike the number 20, 25 was "a perfect square, and symbolizes a quarter of something," he argued. Numbers aside, his heart told him that *The Oprah Winfrey Show* needed to continue. "You've already made history in so many ways, wonderful and beautiful ways, why not make history bigger by having a show with great dignity that touched and inspired so many people for a quarter of a century," he wrote. "I think it's good for the world and good for you. . . . "

Mattie was a philosopher, a prophet, a poet, and a peacemaker, but he was also a child who extolled the virtues of play. An enthusiastic Harry Potter fan, he was very excited when Oprah arranged for him to attend a screening of one of the films and invited him to come on *Oprah* the next day. He was happily surprised when actor Daniel Radcliffe, who plays Harry Potter, walked out on stage (he brought copies of Mattie's books of poetry, which he asked the young writer to sign). Later, Radcliffe and his "Harry Potter" companions, Emma Watson and Rupert Grint, presented Mattie with his very own Harry Potter wand.

Mattie died on June 22, 2004, at the age of thirteen. Former president Jimmy Carter, one of Mattie's heroes, attended his funeral. "We have known kings and queens. We've known presidents and prime ministers, but the most extraordinary person whom I have ever known in my life is Mattie Stepanek," he said. Fittingly, Mattie's legacy—his message of love, peace, hope, and joy—lives on in his books and library dedicated to his memory.

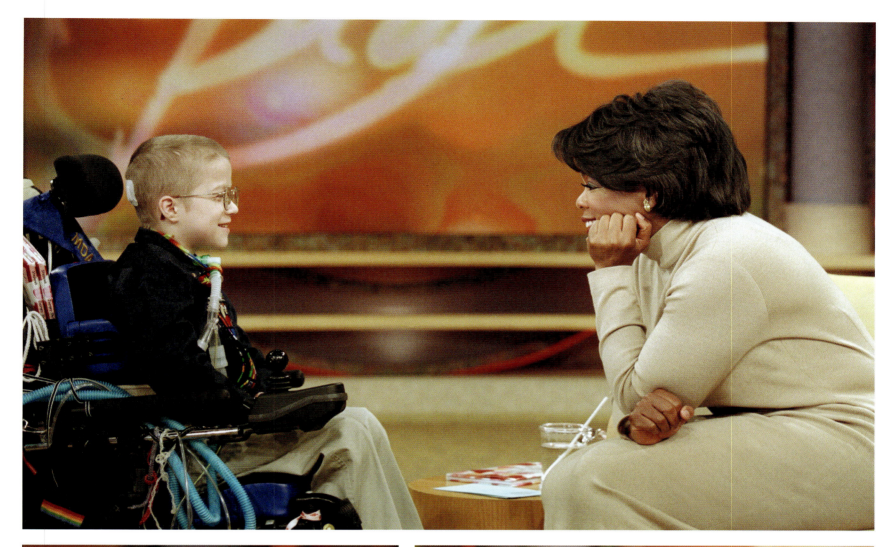

Mattie Stepanek and
Oprah, October 19, 2001.

To: Oprah
From: Mattie
Date: May 14, 2003, 6:57 AM

Dear Oprah,

Hello, it's me, Mattie . . . your guy. I am praying and hoping to go home around Memorial Day. It's not a guarantee, so I am not telling a lot of people. It seems that every time I try to go home, something else goes wrong. The doctors are not able to 'fix' me, but they agree with me going home. and don't worry, I am not 'going home to die' or anything like that. I always live knowing I can die, and probably will die young. But I am going home because they can't do anything else here, and if I heal, it's because I meant to heal, and if I don't heal, then my message is out there and it's time for me to go to Heaven. I personally am hoping that my message still needs me to be the messenger a while longer, but that's really in God's hands. But anyway, I am getting plate- lets every Monday and Wednesday and Friday, and my bleeding has slowed down even though my trachea is still a mess and there is still blood and skin coming out. Also, my blood pressure is becoming more stable and I am needing less fluids to keep my blood pressure up to an okay number. I am only needing red blood cell transfusions about once a week now, so that is better. And it sounds weird, but I think it's really cool that I have blood platelets and red cells and plasma from so many people. Makes me related to the world in some way, which is a proud thing to be.

I know that you are planning to retire your show on its 20th anniversary. It is my opinion that you should wait to stop your daytime show on its 25th anniversary. Let me explain why. 25 makes more sense to me, partially because I'm a bit OCD (obsessive compulsive) and 25 is a perfect number. It's a perfect square, and symbolizes a quarter of something, not just the fifth like the number 20. Also, when I think of the number 25, especially for retiring or completion, or even be- ginning something new, for some reason my mind is filled with bright colors and the rejuvenation of life. I know that sounds weird, but it's true. And you've already made history in so many ways, wonderful and beautiful ways, why not make history bigger by having a show with great dignity that touched and inspired so many people for a quarter of a century. I'll let you think on it. And of course it's only my opinion, but I sometimes get feelings about things, and I have one about this. I think it's good for the world and good for you. . . .

I love you and you love me,
Love, your guy,
Mattie

Mattie
Stepanek

For Our World

We need to stop.
Just stop.
Stop for a moment . . .
Before anybody
Says or does anything
That may hurt anyone else.
We need to be silent.
Just silent.
Silent for a moment . . .
Before we forever lose
The blessing of songs
That grow in our hearts.
We need to notice.
Just notice.
Notice for a moment . . .
Before the future slips away
Into ashes and dust of humility.
Stop, be silent, and notice . . .
In so many ways, we are the same.
Our differences are unique treasures.
We have, we are, a mosaic of gifts
To nurture, to offer, to accept.
We need to be.
Just be.
Be for a moment . . .
Kind and gentle, innocent and trusting,
Like children and lambs,
Never judging or vengeful
Like the judging and vengeful.
And now, let us pray,
Differently, yet together,
Before there is no earth, no life,
No chance for peace.

— Mattie J.T. Stepanek, September 11, 2001

Top: Artworks by Mattie. **Bottom:** Daniel Radcliffe and Mattie, October 29, 2002.

In Good Health

"Embrace the change, no matter what it is; once you do, you can learn about the new world you're in and take advantage of it."

–Nikki Giovanni

The Oprah Winfrey Show spent the majority of its twenty-five years obliterating that line, transforming *us* and *them* into *we*.

In the 1980s, daytime talk shows covered physical, emotional, and psychological problems as if they were a spectator sport. Generally, a guest battling obesity, drug addiction, kleptomania, incest—the more sensational the problem the better—would appear onstage, and the audience, riveted by today's tale of woe, responded with a mixture of sympathy and there-but-for-the-grace-of-God-go-I relief—mostly relief. The guests were perceived as sociological oddities and, at all times, an invisible line separated *us* from *them*.

The Oprah Winfrey Show spent the major-ity of its twenty-five years obliterating that line, transforming *us* and *them* into *we*. On September 12, 1986, during the first week of its inaugural season, the show tackled obe-sity: "How Fat Affects Marriage." Oprah and her guests—several married couples—dis-cussed the strain extra pounds had placed on their relationships. An experienced jour-nalist, Oprah provoked guests and audience members alike to think about the subject in a new way. Did extra weight affect their libidos? And wasn't there a double standard when flabby husbands criticized their wives for los-

ing *their* figures? Oprah had a talent for ask-ing what everyone else was thinking, and her irresistible combination of candor and caring relaxed even the toughest guests. Young, old, quiet, talkative, average, extraordinary—people felt an instant connection with Oprah and they were willing to tell her *everything*.

Oprah wasn't the first talk-show host to project empathy—Phil Donahue, whom she admired, was famous for his sensitivity and warmth—but she somehow managed to be smart host, vulnerable guest, and inquisitive viewer all at once. Furthermore, viewers learned to identify with Oprah's guests because she always managed to put a human face on whatever stories she covered, capturing the essence of the people as well as their problems. Sometimes, that face belonged to Oprah herself.

"I am every one of [my audience] and they are me. That's why we get along so well. I'm vulnerable like them and people say, 'Poor thing. She has big hips, too.'" Starting with her earliest moments on television, Oprah was always honest about her lifelong struggle to control her weight. Like many of her viewers, she gained, she lost, she gained,

Oprah wheels out a red wagon containing 67 pounds of fat, November 15, 1988.

and she lost in her relentless pursuit of a thinner self. Instead of making the subject taboo, or leaving it to the tabloids, she decided to own it. Any serious conversation about Oprah Winfrey's weight, she decided, would be initiated and moderated by Oprah.

Her audience cheered in 1988 when, after enduring a four-month liquid diet, Oprah staged a dramatic, onstage "reveal." She pulled off her coat to unveil a shapely body in a pair of size-10 Calvin Klein jeans. At one point during the show, she wheeled out a little red wagon containing 67 pounds of fat, the equivalent of her weight loss—and tried, but failed, to pick up the hefty bag. "It is amazing to me that I can't lift it but could carry it around every day," she marveled. But her victory over food turned out to be short-lived. A fad diet, Oprah soon discovered, was only a temporary solution. The weight came back as swiftly as it went, and Oprah began to realize that there were bigger issues to be addressed than how many calories to consume in a day.

A year later, the show "Dieting to Death" was revelatory because it moved the conversation about weight in a new direction. Rudine Howard, a twenty-five-year-old

woman suffering from anorexia nervosa, spoke candidly about her life-threatening disease. She weighed only 48 pounds and looked like a skeleton, the barest outline of skin and bone. Yet, incredibly, Howard still believed that she was fat—she admitted that she was incapable of seeing herself as she really was, and her compulsion to be thin was literally killing her. "Thin" was a never-attainable state of mind.

The Oprah Winfrey Show probed the opposite side of America's weight problem—overeating—in an episode titled "Inside the Life of an Obese Person," and did so with great sensitivity and insight. Thirty-one-year-old Stacey Halperin allowed Oprah's cameras to come into her life to witness the sad, hidden world of someone who was morbidly obese. Halperin admitted to weighing 514 pounds. Most days, she stayed at home with the blinds drawn so she would not be depressed by the sight of a world that excluded her. If she did venture out for food, she stayed in her car to shield herself from mocking strangers who made cruel jokes at her expense. She frequented fast food drive-thrus, always adding a second drink to

Bob Greene

A High Altitude Encounter

When I compare my life years ago to my life today, I sometimes think of what would have happened if I hadn't left one of my first jobs out of graduate school. I was the director of the Health & Fitness Institute—a hospital-based wellness program in Florida that offered adult fitness classes, weight-loss programs, cardiac and pulmonary rehabilitation, and physical therapy. I loved my job! I was helping people to change their lives in meaningful ways, which is the passion of most of us in the health-care field. Even to this day, I don't know what possessed me to leave that job and move to the small mountain town of Telluride, Colorado. I did love Telluride, and part of me saw myself living there one day, but to leave a very rewarding career, say good-bye to great friends and colleagues, and move from an area I really liked to run the fitness program for a start-up destination spa—what was I thinking?

As I was setting up the fitness and nutrition department at the spa, there was a mad scramble to open it before the first guests arrived. Four days from opening, the highly qualified trainer I had hired informed me that Telluride was too small for him to move his livelihood there and left town. The next day the general manager said that Oprah was checking in for three weeks and he asked me if I would work with her. While I certainly knew who she was, I didn't own a television and had never seen her show. I don't think I would have recognized her if I saw her at the institute.

On one of the first days I worked with Oprah, we were hiking on a mountain trail. While we were taking a break for lunch, she asked, "So, Bob, where did you grow up?" When I said New Jersey, she replied, "Oh, that's near Stedman!" When I said, "No, you must mean Camden, I don't think there is a Stedman, New Jersey," she dropped her jaw, laughed, and then gave me a look that said *Have you been living under a rock?* You'd be hard-pressed to find two people with more different backgrounds and life experiences, but we hit it off immediately.

Soon after that first meeting in the summer of 1992, her people called and asked if I could come to Chicago and work with her for two months during the off-season. As crazy as this sounds now, I actually had to think about it. After all, I adored living in Telluride. I hiked to work in the summer and skied to work in

the winter, and I never fancied myself much of a city person. But, hey, it was off-season and only for two months, so I packed a few things and drove to Chicago. Two months turned into years. Oprah went from a lifetime high weight of 237 pounds to the perfect weight for her of 148 pounds. She ran several races including a half marathon and a full marathon, which had been a long-standing personal goal of hers. I had appeared on *The Oprah Winfrey Show* a couple of times when she suggested that we should write a book. And we did. After the publication of *Make the Connection* in 1996, my life changed dramatically. I became a more-or-less regular guest on the show. Through Oprah and her producers, I learned, albeit slowly, that you have to entertain people as well as educate them. You have to intrigue people enough so that they will follow up on their own. The show had an amazing ability to take somewhat complex or dry ideas and engage people. People trusted Oprah, and they trusted the show and the experts who appeared on it.

When it comes to the topic of weight loss in particular, the show educated millions of viewers that while it's important to be conscious of what and how they eat and that it is essential to be active, it is their emotions and their lives that need to be managed if they are going to be successful controlling their weight in the long run. The show made it not only acceptable for people to take care of themselves, it taught people that it is one of their primary responsibilities. With *The Oprah Winfrey Show* finishing its twenty-fifth and final season, perhaps the most common question I get asked is: How has the show changed your life? Appearing on *The Oprah Winfrey Show* allowed me to reach millions of people worldwide. It has allowed me to become a best-selling author as well as be a guest on countless other shows. It has allowed me to use my degree and expertise in a very powerful way. More importantly, it has allowed me to help many people change their lives in meaningful ways. But probably the most profound change in my life is how I view the world and my own life since I met Oprah. The show has made me want to be the best I can be, and it has strengthened my desire to be a positive influence on others. What other person could I have bumped into anywhere on the planet who would have had such a profound effect on my life? Absolutely no one.

her enormous order to give the impression that she was buying food for two people.

The show also exposed society's prejudices toward the obese; callous people complained that they were ugly, ignorant, and that they smelled. But Stacey Halperin did not conform to any of these stereotypes. She was an educated woman from a middle-class family. She practiced good hygiene and she cared about the way she looked. Somehow, she had gotten lost in her eating and couldn't find her way back. She was not alone.

Jill Roberts, a twenty-year-old woman who was struggling with her weight, felt betrayed by her family. Her father resented the fact that she was overweight and took the trouble to remind her that she was fat, as if she needed reminding. "Does it bother me when we're out in public that Jill's overweight? It does. I'll be honest," said Kirk, Jill's father. "I'm ashamed of her weight, but I love my daughter dearly," he added. Somehow, it was difficult for Jill to recognize his love, and she suffered terribly as a result.

There was a burgeoning contradiction in America, and it was a dangerous one. Young women like Rudine Howard were falling victim to anorexia at the same time that obesity was on the rise throughout the country. The lesson was that people who starved themselves had something in common with people who overate. Their lives were controlled by their negative relationship with food. *The Oprah Winfrey Show* considered these rapidly spreading eating disorders, whether manifested as obesity or anorexia, to be an important subject for ongoing exploration.

The year 1992 should have been a time of celebration for Oprah. The show's popularity was confirmed when she won her third Emmy for Best Talk Show Host and her fifth for Best Talk Show, but Oprah found herself feeling miserable because, like so many Americans, she had lost control of her weight. Fueled by good intentions, she headed for a health spa in Colorado, where she met fitness expert Bob Greene. She expected Greene, an exercise physiologist and personal trainer, to whip her body into shape with the usual grueling diet and fitness regime. Instead, she was surprised to discover he was more concerned with rehabilitating her spirit. "When was the

Bob Greene in his first appearance on *The Oprah Winfrey Show*, November 22, 1993.

last time you were really happy?" he asked, sensing that something was wrong. The answer was easy: Oprah was happiest when playing Sofia in Steven Spielberg's acclaimed film *The Color Purple*. The harder question to answer was how could she find that happiness again? And what did happiness have to do with weight?

Greene surprised her with his theory that the emotional component of weight loss was equally important as nutrition or exercise. He believed that excess weight was a symbol of something that needed to change. What is it about your life you would alter? he asked his clients. Are you in a toxic relationship? Do you hate what you do for a living? The answer may be different for everyone, he suggested, but he believed it was imperative to connect with that deeper reason, whatever it was.

With Greene's guidance, "Make the Connection" became Oprah's mantra. Thanks to self-reflection, an improved outlook, moderate eating, and a reasonable exercise plan, she gradually became leaner, stronger, and happier. Her crowning moment was running in the arduous Marine Corps Marathon on her fortieth birthday and having the power and stamina to cross the finish line.

Her success was a story worth communicating. But the nature of that communication changed in 1994, when actress Tracey Gold—a recovering anorexic—and Rudine Howard appeared together on *The Oprah Winfrey Show*. At one point, Gold offered her well-intentioned advice for overcoming the disorder they shared. "Make the little steps to fill

Left: Oprah went to New York's Central Park for the last stop on the "Get Movin' with Oprah—Spring Training '95" tour, May 15, 1995.

Right: Oprah takes the stage riding an elephant at the "Spring Training Finale," May 26, 1995.

your mind so that you can fight back," she urged, hoping to inspire Howard to change. Howard considered her words, and then asked, "But *how* do you do it?" Her plaintive question made a tremendous impression on Oprah, who later said, "I realized that we can't just tell people *what* to do, but we have to offer the *how*." This revelation changed the way Oprah approached every show after that. Sadly, it was too late to help Howard, who succumbed to her eating disorder in 1996, weighing only 48 pounds, but Oprah upheld her commitment to use her show to disseminate practical, purposeful, and life-affirming advice and information. Take charge of yourself, was her new philosophy. Be better. Make more intelligent choices. And here's how to do it. In this spirit, *The Oprah Winfrey Show* would offer positive solutions, she resolved, instead of merely calling attention to problems or perpetuating dysfunction.

In 1996, Oprah invited her viewers to experience her new approach to integrated mind/body/spirit well-being. "My weight-loss stories are legendary," she told them, and "if there was any kind of a miracle cure, I would have bought it." But there are no quick fixes, she concluded. Instead, she urged them to "make the connection." Oprah credited Bob Greene with teaching her the value of exercise and

with changing her life as a result. Excited by her enthusiasm, tens of thousands of Americans followed Oprah's lead. "If Oprah can do it, I can do it," they told themselves. They joined her "Get Movin' with Oprah" exercise walks and embraced the Winfrey/Greene *Make the Connection* book and program (although, as the famously wealthy media giant pointed out, she coauthored the book to help people, not to make money), losing an aggregate 534,333 pounds. Oprah celebrated their collective victory by riding an elephant onstage in her "Spring Training Finale."

On another occasion, Oprah took one of her wellness programs out of the studio and directly to the people when she and Bob Greene traveled to Meridian, Mississippi, to launch "Oprah and Bob's Best Life Challenge." Oprah's native Mississippi had been named "the fattest state in the union" for three consecutive years, and she hoped to inspire its portly residents to do something about their unhealthy status. "We are all gathered here today because we are fat," she announced at a town meeting. "Fat" was actually an understatement. One out of three Mississippians was overweight, and many were morbidly obese. The extra weight was life-threatening. Jeff Bailey, who at his highest weight was 771 pounds, had to be hoisted from a hospital

Fans await Oprah and Bob Greene's arrival in Meridian, Mississippi, January 14, 2008.

bed onto a special scale to be weighed. When Oprah asked him how he got to that point, he answered, "I just wouldn't quit eating." Jennifer Marnell weighed 300 pounds, with nowhere to go but up. These determined Mississippians, and others, pledged to follow the "Best Life" diet and lost hundreds of pounds in the process.

David Caruso was an overweight man with a dream—he wanted to sit behind the wheel of a Porsche. But at 525 pounds, it was unlikely that he would be able to squeeze his corpulent body into a tiny sports car. Determined to regain control of his life—and his dreams— Caruso lost more than 300 pounds before appearing on *The Oprah Winfrey Show*. She invited him to sit behind the wheel of a brand-new Porsche—and then let him keep it.

Understanding that wellness was a lifelong pursuit, Oprah carefully assembled a dream team of professionals, beginning with Bob Greene, to teach viewers how to live their best lives. Dr. Mehmet Oz, a professor of surgery at Columbia University and, at the time, director of the Cardiovascular Institute and Complementary Medicine Program at New York–Presbyterian Hospital, made a powerful impression on Oprah and her audience when he first appeared on the show to offer his

unconventional assessment of heart disease. "The heart reflects very closely what's going on spiritually," he suggested. "When you're unhappy at work, with your spouse, in life, when you have no guiding light, it often manifests itself in disease of the heart." On a subsequent show, he talked about the heart being the home of the soul.

Most physicians didn't speak that way. Dr. Oz was a medical doctor with the highest qualifications, yet he believed that the health, or wellness, of the body was linked to something larger than medicine: happiness. The fact that he, like Bob Greene, emphasized the connection between the physical and the spiritual endeared him to Oprah, who pronounced him "America's Doctor." Dapper in his hospital scrubs, he became *The Oprah Winfrey Show*'s resident physician, a smart, straight-talking, compassionate, and empowering MD who banished all traces of fear and mystery from the patient/doctor relationship.

You are in charge of you, he said, providing viewers with the tools they needed to take control of their own well-being. Whether he was teaching them to be cognizant of medical errors (a woman credited Dr. Oz with saving her life because he gave her the confidence to stand up to a doctor who had mishandled her

Opposite, top: Dr. Mehmet Oz and Oprah during a discussion about bowel movements, May 3, 2005.

Opposite, middle: Frank, an audience member, demonstrates for Dr. Oz and Oprah his ability to do push-ups after improving his health, January 6, 2009.

Opposite, bottom: Dan and Shayna discuss their sex life with Dr. Laura Berman and Oprah, April 8, 2010.

double mastectomy and left a tumor in her body), or explaining the importance of self-examinations (a man watching Dr. Oz's show on testicular surgery gave himself one of those exams and detected a life-threatening problem), Dr. Oz made sense. People listened to him. One mention of the virtues of the neti pot, an esoteric device used to flush the sinuses with water, prompted all of America to rush out to buy the Aladdin-like teapots to apply to their noses.

He also had a sense of humor. Dr. Oz shocked—and inspired—men everywhere when he told them matter-of-factly, "If you lose 35 pounds, if you're a male, you gain one inch of penis length," a tip many ecstatic dieters discovered was absolutely true. A conversation about healthy diet led to a lively treatment of a topic so embarrassing no one ever expected to hear it discussed on television: the pursuit of the "perfect poop." Yes, everyone turns around to look at it, Dr. Oz confirmed. No need to be ashamed. Just understand that what goes *in* influences what comes *out*, and eat accordingly.

Another potentially embarrassing subject was intimacy, but Oprah was committed to promoting sexual well-being, and that meant using her show to start a public conversation about sex. "A big part of leading a happier, healthier, and more fulfilling life is good sex," she told her audience. Dr. Laura Berman, a sunny sex therapist with such a wholesome, wholehearted approach to the subject that no one could find her salacious, became *The Oprah Winfrey Show*'s top intimacy expert. She worked with individuals and couples who, hoping to help others, valiantly discussed their sexual problems on the show, from the middle-aged woman who never experienced an orgasm, to the depressed young wife who confessed to having lost all desire.

Oprah's wellness checklist expanded to include economic "health," because money issues could be just as debilitating as those relating to diet or sex. When people couldn't sleep at night, it was usually because they were counting pennies, not calories or conquests. In 2006, *The Oprah Winfrey Show* invited viewers to put themselves on "The Debt Diet," a belt-tightening plan to help families dig themselves out of debt. To enable her

Dr. Mehmet Oz

What Leaders Do

When someone speaks of a mentor, they are referring to someone who usually not only taught them a skill or a philosophy, but who also showed them what they were capable of—often something more than the student had ever envisioned. One of my great mentors, my father-in-law, taught me how to perform heart surgery, how to tread into that twilight between death and life, and delicately coax a heart to beat again. Another mentor, my father, taught me the difference between right and wrong and what was expected of me as a person by leading through example. We all have similar mentors, people we encounter through an accident of birth or academics who bring out the best in us. However, few people have a mentor who has also affected millions, maybe billions, of lives. When I reflect on the way Oprah Winfrey and I met and how we began to work together and the ripple effect it's had—the word *chance* vanishes from my vocabulary to be replaced by its nemesis: *fate*.

I threw myself into medicine as a young and cocky physician. I believed if we pushed science hard enough and I found the right way to explain the secrets of the human body, it was just a matter of time before people everywhere would be healthy. I was wrong—despite staggering discoveries, technologies, and miracle drugs, people were getting sicker. I once operated on a twenty-five-year-old whose lifestyle had contributed to her heart disease only to find her enjoying fast food with her family a day later in the hospital! I went home deep in the cathartic epiphany that no matter how many people I operated on or what device I invented, we weren't making real progress. It was my wife, Lisa, who conceived our first effort on television and thought that maybe by using mass communication to teach more people we could save more lives. Our show, *Second Opinion*, launched on the Discovery Health channel in 2003, and we needed a big name to kick it off. We had nothing to lose, so we made a cold call through Gayle King to ask if Ms. Winfrey would appear. We still laugh at how ridiculous this request must have appeared, but Oprah felt a need deep in her heart to include health in her passionate desire to awaken America. I soon found myself poring over production notes for her first appearance.

A planned ten-minute discussion exploded into more than an hour interview that touched on both her personal health and the greater healing needs of our society. When the series aired, her team invited me on her show as her guest. They didn't give me any hardcore instructions—"just do what you do" seemed to be their message. I showed up in Chicago that first time with a briefcase full of organs from the autopsy lab at New York-Presbyterian Hospital/Columbia University Medical Center, thinking I would show Oprah and the audience what actual disease looked and felt like. The audience was awakened to the impact of our lifestyle choices, and viewers began talking about the organs. I was invited back, and this time we spoke about embarrassing topics such as S-shaped poop that provide vital clues to our health. Soon producers were calling and devoting enormous amounts of effort to the segments. We hit a groove. I became a regular guest, appearing sixty times in seven years before the show ended. In effect, I attended Oprah University.

I think what makes Oprah so unique is that she has so many extraordinary gifts, and yet she is such a regular, ordinary person even with all of her gifts. An audience can watch her and relate to her, and she can empathize with her guests without her success being a barrier. She taught me one of the most valuable lessons I have ever learned: People don't change based on what they know, they change based on how they feel. After all my years of school and time in the operating room, that insight hit me like a bolt of lightning. It didn't matter how well I explained high blood pressure—if I didn't convince you that you'd leave a widow and grieving children from the consequences of it, you'd never take the steps necessary to improve. Oprah knew this intuitively, and she brought a new day to television by showing us what was fascinating about everyday stories. She was making health fascinating and gently waking Americans up to the responsibility they had for their own well-being. I saw this and immediately understood the privilege of being selected as an adjunct on that mission. Oprah was America's principal, and she was letting me teach health class.

As *The Oprah Winfrey Show* sped into its final episodes, thought leaders from all corners tried to crystallize her impact. Consensus centered around a few topics—Oprah had confronted shame in its many forms and had been an advocate for people living with AIDS, survivors of sexual abuse and violence, civil rights for homosexuals, and, of course, race relations. I argue her greatest impact and legacy will be that she made health and wellness "cool." In show after show in those seven years, she made thinking about cholesterol, diabetes, and heart disease seem a natural part of daytime television. The strength I brought to her stage was simply that I had studied these topics and knew the science behind them. Oprah's magic was to find the elusive balance between the gravity of a topic such as colon cancer while allowing the audience to laugh when we talked about the amount of their flatus. No one could have done that, and by doing so, she created a whole new genre in popular television. The critics call it "Medutainment." I call it the missing link that launched a medical renaissance.

Now when I walk through an airport or a public place, people call out to stop me. They never want autographs; they are full of questions about their prescriptions or their loved ones or a medical decision they are facing. After their question, they always refer to something they saw us do that made them laugh: "I remember the show you did on X, and it was so funny." This is how I know we are finally getting through. It was Oprah who taught these kind souls that it was okay to ask their questions and not be embarrassed. It was Oprah who taught me how to listen to them—and I mean really listen—without needing to say anything or succumbing to the urge to fix it. Witnessing and validating their insights and emotions are enough. It was Oprah who taught them and me that humor helps with these tough topics. It makes the reality a little less scary. It makes us feel a little less small. She gave us permission to be us, while making us aware of the responsibility we have to ourselves and our loved ones to take charge of our health.

All of this has become our national conversation on health that she launched with the urgency it deserved and then charged me with carrying on. Every letter we get from a viewer that shares their story of a successful action step, every person that stops me and shares how they got better after hearing or seeing something we did, I trace back to that first invitation to *The Oprah Winfrey Show*. Oprah, my mentor and friend, knew intuitively that we had to talk more about our health, and she set out on that journey with me. The voyage has made an immeasurable impact on our collective well-being and opened up a whole new vista of opportunities. Then again, that's what leaders do.

viewers to achieve an even deeper understanding of money, she subsequently enlisted the help of respected financial adviser and best-selling author Suze Orman. Money, Orman told chronic spendthrifts with her signature tough-love delivery, is never the problem: *You're* the problem because you lack self-esteem. Those who value themselves understand the true value of money.

With Oprah's support, Peter Walsh, an expert in organizational design, extended the concept of wellness to personal space. A home, an office, and even a car served as the objective correlative for a person's state of mind: External clutter reflected internal chaos. The obstacles standing in the way of an organized life, Walsh suggested, were largely emotional. He illustrated his theory in a fascinating episode of *The Oprah Winfrey Show* titled "Inside the Lives of Hoarders." A contemporary malady rooted in runaway consumerism, the hoarding impulse compels people to shop voraciously, to collect compulsively, and to fill their living space with "stuff" that has become an extension of their selves. There was meaning behind their actions. "In buying what we want, we hope to acquire the life we desire," explains Walsh. He taught Sharyn Dorfman, a middle-aged woman who had packed three semitrailers full of belongings (shoes, purses, toys, rolls of wrapping paper) and 75 tons of garbage in a surprisingly small house, to understand that senseless clutter was poisoning her environment and ruining her life. With his help, she learned how to radically edit her hoard and control her impulse to obtain more.

Whether discussing medicine, money, sex, space, or spiritual issues, which became a subject in itself, Oprah's advisers were an all-star team, and they hit a home run when they joined forces in January 2009 for *The Oprah Winfrey Show*'s "Best Life Week." Their approach to wellness was truly "wholistic" because it covered all the important bases with the same underlying philosophy. Fat, debt, sexual dysfunction, clutter, and other debilitating conditions were usually symptoms of underlying problems that stood in the way of happiness and self-fulfillment.

During the five-day series, Oprah and Bob Greene talked about falling off the wagon—

and demonstrated how to climb right back on. Dr. Oz unveiled "The Ultimate Health Checklist," advising men and women to schedule a checkup, to know the five ingredients to avoid (corn syrup, sugar, enriched flour, trans fats, and saturated fats), to learn their critical health numbers (ideal waist size, blood pressure, cholesterol, resting heart rate, blood sugar level, vitamin D level, C-reactive protein, and TSH), and to establish daily goals for exercise and sleep.

Dr. Laura Berman urged couples to put sex at the top of their to-do list and to use their intimate moments together to foster honest communication. Suze Orman also emphasized the importance of honesty. Face up to your money mistakes, she advised, asking

Top: David Bach, Jean Chatzky, and Oprah provide viewers with a step-by-step plan to get out of debt, February 17, 2006.

Bottom: With the support of her family (sons Rich and Steve, daughter Jodi, and husband Marvin), compulsive hoarder Sharyn (second from right) gets advice from Peter Walsh (left) about how to clean out her home and address the deeper issues that have led to her hoarding, November 15, 2007.

everyone in the studio audience (and the viewers at home) to mentally total their credit-card debt and reveal that number to the person next to them. Truth was the precursor to financial recovery, she suggested, and peace of mind would follow. Elizabeth Lesser, the author of *Broken Open: How Difficult Times Can Help Us Grow*, weighed in on spiritual health and well-being. At the end of the week, Oprah's viewers were informed, empowered, and equipped to live their very "best lives."

"Watch Oprah, Get Thin," reported the *Philadelphia Inquirer*. A survey conducted by the website DietSmart.com found that "women who regularly watched the *Oprah*

Top: Suze Orman, January 8, 2009.

Bottom: Leeza Gibbons and Maria Shriver talk with Oprah about their family struggles with Alzheimer's disease, July 13, 2004.

show were seven times less likely to crave fattening foods as women who watch other daytime talkers." This was because they were fed a steady diet of wellness-enhancing information. Over the years, Oprah's ever-expanding circle of experts, including doctors, authors, celebrities, trusted employees, and even friends, was as diverse a group as the health issues they covered.

Oprah's close friend Maria Shriver appeared on the show with television personality Leeza Gibbons to discuss their parents' battles with Alzheimer's disease. Shriver explained that she wrote her book *What's Happening to Grandpa?* to prepare her children for her father's mental and physical deterioration, and discovered that other families desperately needed to learn about compassionate interaction with a loved one who was struck by Alzheimer's.

Preemptive action against diabetes was the topic when Dr. Oz, Bob Greene, diet expert Dr. Ian Smith, and Oprah's chef, Art Smith (a prediabetic who has since lost more than a hundred pounds), joined forces to combat the country's growing diabetes and prediabetes epidemic. Calling the deadly metabolic disease "America's silent killer," they appeared on *The Oprah Winfrey Show* to educate viewers about the dangers of hidden sugars in foods and the need for healthier lifestyles. One of the most shocking revelations was the Centers for Disease Control's pronouncement that half of all African American women born after the year 2000 will develop diabetes in their lifetime. "Diabetes is a ticking time bomb," cautioned Oprah. "It's annihilating the African American community, killing almost a hundred of us every day." There was another concern, Dr. Oz warned. The disease presented catastrophic financial consequences for the country because, with a price tag of $174 billion a year, diabetes was one of its most expensive health issues and could "bankrupt our future ability to pay for health care in the nation."

Michael Pollan, author of such books as *The Omnivore's Dilemma*, *In Defense of Food*, and *Food Rules*, guided viewers on the show "Before You Grocery Shop Again—Food 101 with Michael Pollan," explaining how modern agribusiness has corrupted the food chain,

Michael Pollan, Kathy Freston, Oprah, and director Joe Terry (on screen) talk about going vegan for a week, February 1, 2011.

and warning that the foods we eat bear little resemblance to the foods consumed by our ancestors. The antidote to our compromised food supply was to return to the land: to get out of the supermarkets and support local farmers. "Eat food—mostly plants—not too much," Pollan advised.

Veganist and author Kathy Freston seconded that motion when she led 378 Harpo employees in their attempt to go vegan for one week, a challenge which prohibited eating meat, fish, dairy, eggs—anything that comes from an animal. One video editor who usually feasted on a sausage muffin and a huge coffee with five creams every day discovered that eliminating animal from his diet made him feel better than he had in ten years. He also shed eleven pounds. Whether or not Oprah's staff lost weight during the vegan challenge, they—and the show's audience—gained awareness and an alternate point of view. Because of their experiences, they would never look at food the same way.

For twenty-five years, *The Oprah Winfrey Show* has explored a full panoply of mind-expanding and life-altering health issues, and Oprah herself has unashamedly shared the vicissitudes of her personal journey to wellness with her viewers. One of the reasons weight has been a recurring theme is because the topic reveals so much about

human frailty and, conversely, human resilience and resolve. Whatever the obstacles, people really do want to be better. For Oprah, there have been many highs and lows on the road to wellness: the triumph of appearing in exercise clothes on the cover of *Shape Magazine* in 1996, and the embarrassment of acknowledging that she had fallen off the wagon on the cover of *O, The Oprah Magazine* in 2008. But Oprah shared her very human struggle for the greater good. What she learned, even in failure, helped her audience to become informed, and motivated *them* to work toward better health.

"Thank you, Oprah," viewers wrote, sending in heartfelt letters and emails about the wellness lessons they learned on *The Oprah Winfrey Show*. Some episodes imparted valuable information. "I recently noticed that my 7 year old grandson was reading food labels and making wise choices," a grandmother wrote. "I asked him how he knew so much about reading food labels. He told me that he watches Oprah." A single mother of three who was drowning in debt credited *Oprah* with giving her the tools she needed to reclaim her life. "I watched your Debt Diet series a few years ago. At that time I had more than $30,000 in credit card debt," she wrote. She was proud to say that "as of today I made my final credit card payment. I am

Oprah and the ultimate
viewers who each lost over
100 pounds, May 10, 2011.

COMPLETELY CREDIT CARD DEBT FREE." And a public-health educator and HIV/STD counselor took the time to write, "You've done great work to reduce the stigma attached to HIV, promote testing, and applaud prevention. On behalf of the women you motivated to get tested in my clinic, I thank you."

Some viewers said that watching a particular show saved their lives, or saved the life of a loved one. A grateful woman wrote, "In early June of 2001, one of the ladies in your audience thanked you for having a show on breast cancer. I was sitting on my couch watching your show . . . and just automatically reached up to check. I was shocked to find a large mass that was big enough to feel through my clothes and bra. If you hadn't had that show on that day, I have no idea how long it might have been before it was discovered."

A woman who watched a show on hormones said in an email, "I started to cry because everything the women were saying described how I was feeling. . . . I immediately contacted a doctor. . . . He said I had the functioning body of a 70 year old woman. I am 57. To know that this could be ending soon is like a miracle in my life." A daughter wrote that Oprah saved her ninety-two-year-old mother by outlining the symptoms of heart attack in women. And a mother who was having a tough time with her daughter tried Oprah's anger exercises and thanked her for doing "more in an hour than 2 years of family therapy . . . You saved us both and started the healing of a strained, disgruntled, and explosive relationship." One enthusiastic viewer summarized her feelings—and what other viewers often felt—by writing, "Oprah, I have been trying for weeks to think about specifics about how your show has changed my life. What has changed? Only EVERYTHING."

The important goal, viewers learned with Oprah over time, was not to obsess over a particular weight, or conform to a certain body image or health profile, but to steadfastly pursue *balance* in every aspect of their physical, mental, and spiritual lives—a way of honoring themselves. When you fill yourself, you have more to give to others. This lesson is perhaps *The Oprah Winfrey Show*'s greatest wellness legacy.

Here's to Books

"Read, read, read.
Read everything."

–William Faulkner

"What we want to do is start a book club here on the *Oprah* show. I want to get the whole country reading again."

Oprah Winfrey has always loved books. She learned how to read at the age of three, and when she was a little girl growing up in Mississippi, books transported her to the world beyond her grandmother's front porch. She was surprised to discover that not everyone had an outhouse, or was poor—that life had possibilities. Books were her friends when she was lonely, and a personal sanctuary—a place for retreat, contemplation, and self-reflection—in the midst of chaos, hardship, even adversity. They inspired her to do better—to *be* better. At school, when she was assigned to kindergarten instead of the more advanced class she knew she deserved, she wrote an indignant note to her teacher: "Dear Miss Newe, I do not belong here, because I can read and I know a lot of big words: elephant, hippopotamus." Thanks to her confidence (and her impressive vocabulary), Oprah was promoted to the first grade the very next day. There was a whole new universe out there, and it was hers at the turn of a page. Books could open doors, awaken the imagination, and touch the heart.

As an adult—and a busy and successful one at that—Oprah always made time for reading.

Oprah's first-grade school photo, approximately age six.

Oprah announces her first Book Club selection, *The Deep End of The Ocean* by Jacquelyn Mitchard, September 17, 1996.

"I'm the girl under the tree with a book," she joked, when describing her ideal vacation. At work, she and her friend Alice McGee, a producer for *The Oprah Winfrey Show*, would trade books and engage in passionate discussions about their favorite titles. They didn't always agree, but their conversations heightened their enjoyment and deepened their understanding of whatever it was they were reading. One day, Oprah decided to share those spirited book discussions with her other friends—millions of them.

"This is one of my all-time favorite moments I'm having on television right now," Oprah told her audience on September 17, 1996. "What we want to do is start a book club here on the *Oprah* show. I want to get the whole country reading again." Her inaugural selection was *The Deep End of the Ocean* by first-time novelist Jacquelyn Mitchard. Viewers could buy the book or borrow it from a library. (Subsequently, starting in November 1996, the show asked each publisher to donate ten thousand copies to the American Library Association for libraries throughout the country.) There was an allotted time period, in this case, one month, and readers who enjoyed it—as well as those who didn't—were invited to express their opinions in letters. A select few would be invited to join Oprah and the author for a televised discussion the following month.

It was an ambitious—even risky—endeavor. The prevailing wisdom in the media business was that people who watched television, especially daytime television, did not read books. Oprah never underestimated her viewers, but she did have some reservations about the idea. There was no guarantee that the books *she* enjoyed reading would appeal to anyone else. And it would be a tremendous challenge to turn a book discussion into lively, effective, don't-change-that-channel television. "I thought we would die in the ratings," she confessed. However, this venture wasn't about business; it was about awakening the show's vast audience to the pleasures of reading. Doubts aside, Oprah launched her Book Club because she believed in the power of the word.

She also believed in authors and wanted to give viewers unprecedented access to the men and women who write books. A self-

described author "groupie," Oprah often reached out to writers to praise their work. After reading *The Deep End of the Ocean*, she left not one, but *three* admiring messages on Jacquelyn Mitchard's answering machine before receiving a call back. In fact, Mitchard assumed that the persistent caller was either a crank or a friend pretending to be Oprah Winfrey as a prank.

The publication of *The Deep End of the Ocean* marked a turning point in Mitchard's life. After her husband died of cancer, the financially challenged mother of four realized that she would have to abandon her dream of becoming a full-time writer to pursue a more practical and lucrative course. But Mitchard followed her heart instead of her head, and started writing the compelling story of a kidnapping—a mother's horrific loss—and the miraculous reunion and healing that occurs nine years later. She was fortunate enough to sell her manuscript to Viking Books and saw it debut to favorable reviews and solid sales. Then there was *The Oprah Winfrey Show*. Immediately after the novel was announced as the Book Club's first pick, the title shot to the top of fiction best-seller lists including the *New York Times*.

When the first Book Club discussion aired in October of 1996, viewers proved that they

had been busy reading. They wrote impassioned letters expressing their feelings about Oprah's selection. "I had to read this book under the covers with a flashlight so my husband could sleep," said one woman. "I am 46 years old. And until this past year, I have not read more than five books," admitted another. Some readers were inspired to kiss their children after experiencing the harrowing tale of kidnapping. One bride-to-be even wondered whether parenthood was right for her. "I'm getting married in December, and it—it made me question whether or not I really want to be a parent right now. Am I capable of protecting a child at this point in my life?" she asked.

Four readers were invited to join Oprah and Jacquelyn Mitchard for the Book Club's first televised dinner with an author, an evening of fine food and spirited conversation. Whether they were troubled or inspired, angry or enthusiastic, viewers were eager to be a part of this exciting new literary community. Oprah's Book Club was off to a smashing start. "Here's to books!" she toasted.

Oprah's surprising second selection, a book written by Nobel and Pulitzer Prize winner Toni Morrison, signaled that she had something else up her sleeve: high expectations. Yes, she wanted her viewers to read,

Oprah invites Jacquelyn Mitchard (far left) to the first Book Club dinner to discuss *The Deep End of the Ocean*, October 18, 1996.

but she also expected them to stretch, to challenge themselves. "I feel passion for this author," she said. "With no disrespect to all the other books and authors I've read, I believe that she is the greatest living American author, male or female, white or black. And she is, of course, Toni Morrison." *Song of Solomon* was Oprah's choice, and it came with a caveat. "I just encourage you to stay with Ms. Morrison. Put your trust in her because she knows what she's doing . . . you'll find that you need to sometimes reread a page." In fact, Oprah herself was a little lost when she first read the novel. "I called up Toni Morrison and asked, 'Do people tell you they have to keep going over the words sometimes?'" "*That*, my dear, is called reading," was Morrison's wise reply.

For the *Song of Solomon* Book Club "meeting," Oprah invited four "great and lucky" readers, as she described them, to come to her home for an intimate dinner and book discussion with Morrison. One of those chosen, an affluent white professional, wrote, "I've never been black; I've never been poor; I've never been abused. So what could I have in common with this odd group of characters? Too much, way too much," she was surprised to discover. A stay-at-home mom wrote, "I just closed that book and I said,

'I have got to see the person who wrote that. I've just got to see her.'"

Oprah was equally excited by the prospect of spending an evening with her favorite author, and fussed over every detail, including buying brand-new china for the literary giant. Morrison did not disappoint. The dinner participants—and later, the studio audience—were spellbound by her warmth, her wisdom, and her willingness to share her innermost feelings about both writing and life. "Oh, I love to hear it when they say this remarkable thing, 'I had to read every word,'" Morrison told the group. "And I always wanted to say, 'Yeah—and I had to write every word.'" The discussion provoked tears, revelations, and epiphanies. And when it was over, *Song of Solomon* was more than a book: It was an exciting journey to self-discovery.

With its first two selections, Oprah's Book Club awakened readers to the importance of story and storytelling. Her fourth selection, Wally Lamb's *She's Come Undone*, introduced them to character. And what a powerful and endearing character she was. Dolores Price was Everywoman—any woman who had ever endured pain and degradation, and then looked deep into herself to find the courage, heart, humor, and indomitable sprit to survive. Lamb was every bit as charismatic as his heroine. Oprah loved the fact that the first time she called the teacher/novelist and father of three at his home in Connecticut to say how much she enjoyed his book he was doing the family laundry. *Authors do laundry*, she marveled.

Oprah's Book Club was up and running, and publishers who were indifferent, cynical, or even suspicious at the outset realized that becoming one of her book selections was the equivalent of winning the literary lottery. Authors who received the coveted call were sworn to secrecy. Their publishers hurriedly produced and shipped hundreds of thousands of Oprah's Book Club copies of the lucky book, which arrived at stores in unmarked cartons (booksellers did not know what they had ordered), ready for the big reveal. "Once the announcement is made, it's like a tidal wave," marveled a publicist at Simon and Schuster. "All we can do is get out of the way." That tidal wave consistently

Wally Lamb and Oprah, February 28, 1997.

propelled each title to the top of the best-
seller list, promoting phenomenal sales.
"The best thing to happen to the publishing
industry since paper," proclaimed the
Boston Globe.

The gold rush continued, as each announcement triggered a stampede to the bookstore.
Smart customers learned to avoid Barnes &
Noble the day after a new selection was
unveiled because the parking lot would be
jammed. But announcing the title was only
the beginning of the Book Club's monthly
sprint to showtime. Oprah's producers had to
find ways to make each choice an interesting
and engaging television experience. Their
imaginations ran wild, and viewers learned
to expect the unexpected.

To fully experience the power and intimacy
of the Book Club's seventh selection, Maya
Angelou's *The Heart of a Woman,* Oprah
and her readers visited the legendary author
at her home, where she prepared smothered
chicken and biscuits for dinner. "A half a
biscuit has never hurt a soul," Angelou
assured Oprah as she passed her a tray of
freshly baked ones. Later, the group settled
in for an after-hours pajama party, complete
with special Book Club pajamas. The atmo-
sphere that evening was so personal and
familial that it encouraged Oprah, her guests,
and Maya Angelou herself, to speak from
the heart. One woman, a teacher named
Beth Alexander, thanked the writer for saving
her life; she was sexually abused by a family
member when she was thirteen, and her one
source of strength and solace was her worn
copy of Angelou's masterpiece, *I Know Why
the Caged Bird Sings,* which she kept hidden
under her bed. "As I read her story, I found
someone who understood my feelings,"
Alexander recounted. "Our experiences were
different, but the feelings were the same.
She knew me even though we had never
met. I clung to that book like it was my lifeline. She understood my terror, my pain, my
fear of telling anyone what was happening
to me. I know it to the core of my soul that
Dr. Angelou's book kept me alive."

Deeply felt revelations such as this suggested that Oprah's readers were ready to
experience new levels of engagement. In
addition to illustrating the scope and variety
of the outside world, books could illuminate

Top: Oprah's Book Club members, Maya Angelou, and Oprah discuss *The Heart of a Woman* during a pajama party at Angelou's house, June 18, 1997.

Bottom: Ursula Hegi and Oprah, April 8, 1997.

important issues. Ursula Hegi's *Stones from the River* recounted the horrors of Nazi Germany through the eyes of a heroic outsider, a librarian who was a dwarf. *A Lesson Before Dying*, Ernest J. Gaines's poignant and powerful novel about a young black man unjustly condemned to death row and his life-altering (and affirming) relationship with his teacher, inspired Oprah to take her readers to the Riverlake Plantation in Louisiana, the place where Gaines was born and raised, and where he set his novel. With the author as their guide, Oprah and four readers visited the locations that were meaningful to Gaines when he was growing up, including the slave cemetery, the old schoolroom, and, most importantly, the Big House, which was off-limits to blacks when he lived there. When Oprah asked Gaines if he had even dreamed of crossing its threshold, he said he didn't think it was even a possibility in his lifetime. Therefore, it was a profound moment when he was served dinner in the dining room. The group discussed everything from race to Gaines's writing process. "The object of writing," he suggested, "should be to create characters with character to help others develop their character."

Black and Blue, Anna Quindlan's riveting portrayal of a battered wife, inspired a similarly emotionally charged discussion. The book encouraged readers to open their eyes to the silently suffering women in their lives—relatives, friends, and neighbors who were victimized by their spouses. At Rainbow House, a shelter for abused women, battered wives candidly tried to explain their complicated reasons for not leaving a destructive relationship. Many had practical concerns about their children and their financial security, but most were paralyzed by fear. They were afraid to stay, but even more afraid to go. One reader named Catherine, the seemingly privileged wife of an affluent surgeon, said that she finally found the nerve to call 911 to report her husband's abuse while she was holding *Black and Blue* in her hand—proving that a book *could* change the course of a life.

For her dedicated readers, Oprah was coach and cheerleader rolled into one. "Don't be intimidated," she told them, and they listened. They read Toni Morrison's *Paradise* and, when

For her dedicated readers, Oprah was coach and cheerleader rolled into one. "Don't be intimidated," she told them, and they listened.

Ernest J. Gaines and Oprah visit Riverlake Plantation in Pointe Coupee Parish, Louisiana, where Gaines was born and raised, October 27, 1997.

Toni Morrison

A Radical Gift

For me, *The Oprah Winfrey Show* was always interesting and often compelling. But then it became radical—in the best sense of that term. When Oprah asked her television audience to turn off the television now and then and read a book, one she had selected because it interested her, it was a genuine revolution. Not only because it encouraged buying and reading books, not only because the chosen books became topics of serious conversation.

I have spent all of my life reading books, teaching books, editing books, and writing them. While teaching books, I know that students in my classes expect a grade on their interpretative prowess, so they dearly want the right interpretation, the approved, even sophisticated, view. They may not trust their own judgments and struggle for language to conform to the judgments of others: critics, book reviewers, scholars, professors. But Oprah's program liberated the reader to enjoy or be disappointed by or quarrel with the author/narrator without fear of being wrong. The book belonged to the reader and s/he owned her or his own evaluation of it.

That is precisely what free engagement with a text provides: the lifting of a lid under which the imaginations of both writer and reader merge or part.

I still don't know if Oprah realizes how powerful what she ignited has been. Of course, she knows it "worked." She is herself an avid reader, hungry for books and the language to describe them and their meaning. She gave her audience the gift she herself treasured—which is the rare and sacred aspect of gift giving.

Clearly there are many other instances of generosity on her show. Yet there is another quality that distinguishes *The Oprah Winfrey Show*. I have a friend whose mother is a faithful, even obsessive, viewer of the show. For her, nothing can interfere with tuning in. Her daughter once questioned her mother's passion (there were other shows, yes?). Her mother's answer was: "No matter the topic, I always know more and feel better at the close of Oprah's show."

Simple. Profound.

they needed help navigating the book's complex structure and themes, Oprah arranged for a master class at Princeton University, taught by the author herself.

Each month, they looked at the world through the eyes of extraordinary characters who were light years away from the lives they knew, from the vulnerable, yet resilient, teenager in Janet Fitch's *White Oleander*, to the Belgian Congo missionaries in Barbara Kingsolver's *The Poisonwood Bible*, and the disturbing—and disturbed—narrators in Christina Schwartz's *Drowning Ruth*. Bill Cosby hosted a wacky book party for kids, beloved author Wally Lamb returned with his new work, *I Know This Much Is True*, and Isabel Allende shared her innermost feelings about her daughter's death and the mystical process of writing while discussing her novel *Daughter of Fortune*. Rohinton Mistry, the author of *A Fine Balance*, created an epic tale of modern-day India in all of its extraordinary variety.

Most authors fantasized about receiving the fateful call informing them that their work had been selected for Oprah's Book Club, but one writer was surprisingly—and very publicly—conflicted when the call actually came. In 2001, Jonathan Franzen's novel *The Corrections* debuted to rave reviews, healthy sales, and an invitation to be the Book Club's forty-third selection. Franzen accepted, all the while ruminating on whether or not it was a good idea to align his book with Oprah's audience. He found some of her choices "schmaltzy," he said in an interview, and they made him "cringe." After hearing Franzen's reservations, Oprah withdrew her invitation, saying, "He is seemingly uncomfortable and conflicted about being chosen as a Book Club selection. It is never my intention to make anyone uncomfortable or cause anyone conflict."

The Franzen fracas aside, Oprah's readers were enthusiastic members of an ever-expanding Book Club community, publishers and bookstores were thriving, and libraries all over America were the happy beneficiaries of hundreds of thousands of books. The literary journey continued. With *We Were the Mulvaneys*, Joyce Carol Oates transported readers deep into the heart of the American psyche. Malika Oufkir, author of *Stolen Lives: Twenty Years in a Desert Jail*, told the harrow-

Top: Book Club discussion of Toni Morrison's *Paradise* at Princeton University, March 6, 1998.

Bottom: Bill Cosby signs a copy of one of his books for D'Andre, after the Book Club dinner, January 16, 1998.

ing story of her family's fall from grace in Morocco and the twenty-four-year imprisonment that followed. Books were back, it seemed, and in a big way, until suddenly, and without warning, it stopped.

On April 5, 2002, Oprah made a startling announcement. "I just want to say that this is the end of the Book Club as we know it. . . . From now on when I come across something I feel absolutely compelled to share, I will do that, but it will not be every month. The truth is it has just become harder and harder for me to find books on a monthly basis that I really am passionate about." Readers were upset because they looked forward to Oprah's selections. "The people at the bookstore were waiting for me with the new selection every month when it came out," a disappointed fan named Lori recalled. "I just—I live for the book club." But if readers were despondent, publishers and booksellers were absolutely devastated. As an editor in chief of *Publishers Weekly* noted in an interview, every title Oprah picked moved at least six hundred thousand to eight hundred thousand additional copies after being selected. No one else had that power. Lightning would not strike again, industry insiders lamented.

But they underestimated the power of the word. During a summer vacation, Oprah read a novel that was so compelling—so impossible to put down—that she wished she still had a Book Club. A few months later, she made that wish become a reality. "I am on a mission," she told her excited fans. The Book Club was back but, this time, the selections would be classics. The page-turner that inspired the return was John Steinbeck's *East of Eden,* and it would be the first of many great books—and even greater experiences—to come.

Alan Paton's *Cry, the Beloved Country,* a powerful tale of the roots of South African apartheid, was the next classic. The novel's setting was so magnificent that *The Oprah Winfrey Show* was inspired to fly three ecstatic readers 8,700 miles to see Paton's landscape firsthand. Cameras followed them from one end of South Africa to another, from Johannesburg to Soweto to Cape Town, enabling viewers to share their transforming "trip of a lifetime."

Top: Malika Oufkir, June 20, 2001.

Middle: A discussion of Rohinton Mistry's *A Fine Balance*, January 24, 2002.

Bottom: Oprah goes to Naperville, Illinois, to sign people up for the Book Club and give out the new Book Club selection, June 18, 2003.

Classics, Oprah's readers discovered, could be challenging. Gabriel García Márquez's *One Hundred Years of Solitude* taught them to appreciate magic realism, while Pearl S. Buck's *The Good Earth*, an award-winning story of China before the 1949 Revolution, connected readers to a shocking issue in contemporary China—baby girls who are abandoned, neglected, and even murdered because of their gender. Book Club members powered their way through a marathon reading of all 817 pages of Tolstoy's *Anna Karenina* (chanting "Anna, Anna, Anna" as they reached the finish line). They also spent a summer tackling not one but *three* difficult books by William Faulkner: *As I Lay Dying*, *The Sound and the Fury*, and *Light in August*. "If you have not read this author, you cannot say that you have been baptized as a real reader," Oprah said when she unveiled this selection. Recognizing that Book Club members might need a little help, the show instituted "Oprah's Classroom," a weekly online-video-lecture series featuring discussions by leading Faulkner scholars. "You are a real reader now," she congratulated them at the end of that summer, "because if you can read Faulkner, you can read anything." Every month, more and more readers embraced the challenge, and an appreciative *New York Times* called Oprah's Book Club "a wonder, the equivalent of a course in one of the 20th century's great novels."

Oprah's Book Club changed direction again in September 2005, and the reason this time was not a classic, but a classic page-turner: *A Million Little Pieces*. Oprah confessed to staying up for two nights straight when she announced the latest selection to the studio audience, describing it as "a gut-wrenching memoir that is raw and . . . so real. It's a wild ride through addiction and rehab that has been called electrifying, intense, mesmerizing, and even gruesome. It's a radical departure. It's not a classic, and it is also not fiction." It was author James Frey's enthralling personal story and, she promised, "You'll zip through it."

And zip through it they did. Readers who identified with Frey's problems called the book their lifeline and embraced his "just hold on" message as their mantra. Those who had no personal experience with addiction were mesmerized by the power and nail-biting tension of Frey's recollections. Someone wrote, "It hurt my head and stretched my brain. The truth took on a new meaning for me. I will make decisions now and just hold on. I didn't know how badly I needed this message."

"Truth" was the word that won over a million fans, and "truth" was the word that confused and ultimately alienated them. At the height of his Oprah-fueled success, Frey was accused of embellishing the "facts" in his book, of writing more fiction than memoir. Initially, Oprah

Oprah confronts James Frey about embellishing parts of *A Million Little Pieces*, January 26, 2006.

Elie Weisel, accompanied by Oprah in January 2006, made what he would call his final trip to the Auschwitz death camp in Poland, May 24, 2006.

supported him, saying that his "underlying message of redemption" still resonated with her and that she relied on his publishers "to define the category that a book falls within and also the authenticity of the work."

However, when Oprah realized that Frey's publisher had not vetted his work, and that he had completely fabricated some of the most significant details and episodes in his book, she had to assume the role of advocate for her readers. "I left the impression that the truth does not matter. And I am deeply sorry about that, because that is not what I believe," she stated forcefully during a televised encounter with Frey and his editor. Truth matters, especially in a *memoir*, she insisted—otherwise, write a novel. The lesson? Discerning readers must hold authors and their publishers accountable for the honesty of their works.

The controversy surrounding *A Million Little Pieces* was fierce and ongoing, but several months later, Oprah's fifty-fifth Book

Club selection was a memoir so unassailable, with a message so pure and powerful, that she hoped it "would be engraved on every human heart." The book was *Night*, Nobel Peace Prize winner Elie Wiesel's shattering, *true* account of the horrors he witnessed as a young boy at Auschwitz during the Holocaust. "These 120 pages I'm about to tell you about should be required reading for all humanity," she said. Oprah accompanied Professor Wiesel to the death camp in Poland, where they retraced his steps—from the barrack where he fought his daily battle for survival to the crematorium where he lost his mother and sister—and viewers were able to see the Holocaust through the eyes of a man who lived it.

It was Oprah's hope that young people would read along with her, so she also announced the first "Oprah's National High School Essay Contest." Students were invited to answer the question, "Why is Elie Wiesel's book *Night* relevant today?" Fifty winners were selected from approximately fifty

thousand submissions (a response so overwhelming that the show had to recruit local high school teachers to help read the essays), and were flown to Chicago to appear on television.

Readers tore through Sidney Poitier's *The Measure of a Man,* Cormac McCarthy's *The Road* (and witnessed the author's first-ever television interview), Gabriel García Márquez's *Love in the Time of Cholera,* Jeffrey Eugenides's *Middlesex,* and Ken Follett's *The Pillars of the Earth.* Then, on March 3, 2008, the show hosted its first worldwide webinar in tandem with what proved to be its biggest Book Club selection, *A New Earth* by spiritual leader Eckhart Tolle. "Just the most exciting thing I've ever done," Oprah said about the Internet event, inviting readers to join her and the renowned author for a free, multipart, live interactive webinar on Oprah .com. Penguin Group, the book's publisher, shipped 3.45 million copies in the four-week period following the announcement, and more than 500,000 people—representing 125 countries— registered. During the first webinar, the number of registrants shot up toward a million, and the overloaded server crashed as excited staffers watched the population of their online community explode. By using this platform, *The Oprah Winfrey Show* extended its reach around the globe.

Ironically, after introducing readers to the newest technology, Oprah later announced

that she was going "old school" for her final book selection on *The Oprah Winfrey Show*. Charles Dickens's *A Tale of Two Cities* and *Great Expectations* were her choices. She had never read Dickens and planned on experiencing his works for the first time along with her readers. Not surprisingly, after Oprah's endorsement, the 198-year-old author—and his books—were suddenly hot.

A publishing insider credited Oprah's Book Club with generating a remarkable $500 million in sales ($100 million for Random House, alone). People listened to her—they faithfully bought the titles she recommended and, according to Barnes & Noble, 75 percent of these newly impassioned readers purchased an additional book while they were in the store. "There's never been anyone like Oprah who could galvanize a mass audience to embrace serious literature," said an executive at Simon & Schuster. "She's brought unparalleled excitement and attention to books. All of America should be grateful to her," enthused Jane Friedman, president and CEO of HarperCollins Publishers and vice chair of the Association of American Publishers.

The authors of the books selected by the literary tastemaker had their own stories to tell about the "Oprah Effect" on their lives, and, amazingly, the phenomenal royalties they collected were not always foremost in their minds. "I still drive an old clunker of a car," two-time Oprah pick Wally Lamb liked to joke when journalists asked about his double windfall. He subscribed to Oprah's philosophy that the key to success is to take what you need and pass on the rest to others. Inspired, he taught a writing class at a women's prison and watched proudly as one of his students went on to win a PEN Award. Joyce Carol Oates said, "My Book Club Experience was a highpoint of my writing life." She loved the readers and found them "serious, thoughtful," and "emotionally engaged." "I don't think anyone has done more for what words and reading and books can mean to our culture than Oprah Winfrey," praised Chris Bohjalian, author of *Midwives*.

But happy publishers, authors, and bookstores notwithstanding, the most important beneficiaries of Oprah's Book Club were her readers. Every time she announced a title, Oprah encouraged them to be curious and to express their opinions with a strong, confident voice. When she called reading "the single greatest pleasure I have," others listened and followed her example. "You have inspired me to find time to return to reading once again. I found myself poring over the books that you recommended, something I had not done for many years," offered a fan from Michigan. "I feel like you have chosen these books just for me," emailed a young mother who curled up with an Oprah book each night after her daughter fell asleep. "Thank you, Oprah, for inspiring me to become a more literate person," was a sentiment repeated by countless readers.

Oprah said that she considered her Book Club to be one of her greatest achievements. Better than an Emmy, in fact. It was so meaningful to her to watch "somebody who hasn't picked up a book since they were forced to in high school to read *Song of Solomon* and start thinking differently about their own life as a result." For her, it was all about igniting a passion for books. For fifteen years and sixty-five selections, Oprah's Book Club spotlighted literary superstars and talented unknowns, best sellers, discoveries, and beloved classics. What started out as an "all-time-favorite moment," a dream, even, went on to become nothing less than the biggest book club in the world.

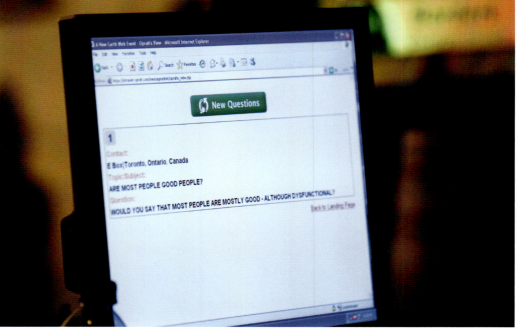

In a live webinar, Eckhart Tolle and Oprah discuss *A New Earth* and take questions from participants, March 3, 2008.

Elie Wiesel

Oprah's Silence

It was dense, intense, not as when you have nothing to say but when there is too much to be said. When pain is so deep that only silence can contain and express its unique truth.

Auschwitz. Birkenau. A freezing day in January. We had a date there.

Whose idea was it? Mine? Hers? It just came to us while we were talking about my testimony. At one point, I said that, tragically, the experience of what we so poorly call the "Holocaust" cannot be communicated. The enemy succeeded in pushing his crimes to the limits of language and beyond. Ask any survivor and he or she will respond that "You will not understand, because there are no words for it."

Probably it was her sadness that moved me to say: "One day we shall go there together."

Scheduling difficulties. Not easy to find three consecutive days and nights. I was expected at the World Economic Forum in Davos. I could only go to Cracow for one day. Problem: That day was her birthday.

One of the most admired women in the world canceled her personal celebrations. In Cracow, we stayed at the same hotel. I thought we would meet immediately, the evening I arrived. No: She did not wish to talk before. Before we entered that place. She wanted to meet at the Auschwitz gate and enter the camp together. The first words—hers and mine—were to be uttered inside. The visit was meant not to be a spectacle but an experience. No press, no television, no media. No officials were to accompany us.

Marching in the snow, from one barrack to another, Oprah at first looked bewildered. When I glanced at her as we walked past the gas chambers, the mountains of hair, the thousands of eyeglasses, the suitcases with name tags, she looked ashen.

More than a million Jews—men, women, and children—had been brought here forcibly from all over Europe, condemned to extermination not because of what they had done or said, but because of what and who they were: To be Jewish had become a crime to be punished by torture and death.

I whispered to Oprah that in 1944 when it was the turn of Hungarian Jews, my Hungarian Jews, to face death, the SS decided that there were too many of us for the overcrowded crematoria. A solution was found: They lit gigantic fires in the trenches. And in the end, they threw babies into the flames alive.

Oprah was crying silently.

A silence filled with sorrow. She didn't speak.

Later, millions of people in America and elsewhere watched and listened as she remembered her visit to Auschwitz.

If *Night*, my memoir, is now being read and studied by more and more students in high schools and colleges, it is because she put it in their hands. Her commitment to memory and truth encouraged her followers—and they are legion—to attempt to bring sanity to a world threatened by indifference and evil.

Oprah's Book Club

1996

1997

1998

1999

2000

1996

The Deep End of the Ocean
Jacquelyn Mitchard

Song of Solomon
Toni Morrison

The Book of Ruth
Jane Hamilton

1997

She's Come Undone
Wally Lamb

Stones from the River
Ursula Hegi

The Rapture of Canaan
Sheri Reynolds

The Heart of a Woman
Maya Angelou

Songs in Ordinary Time
Mary McGarry Morris

A Lesson Before Dying
Ernest J. Gaines

Ellen Foster
A Virtuous Woman
Kaye Gibbons

The Meanest Thing to Say
The Treasure Hunt
The Best Way to Play
Bill Cosby

1998

Paradise
Toni Morrison

Here on Earth
Alice Hoffman

Black and Blue
Anna Quindlen

Breath, Eyes, Memory
Edwidge Danticat

I Know This Much Is True
Wally Lamb

*What Looks Like Crazy
on an Ordinary Day*
Pearl Cleage

Midwives
Chris Bohjalian

Where the Heart Is
Billie Letts

1999

Jewel
Bret Lott

The Reader
Bernhard Schlink

The Pilot's Wife
Anita Shreve

White Oleander
Janet Fitch

Mother of Pearl
Melinda Haynes

Tara Road
Maeve Binchy

River, Cross My Heart
Breena Clarke

Vinegar Hill
A. Manette Ansay

A Map of the World
Jane Hamilton

2000

Gap Creek
Robert Morgan

Daughter of Fortune
Isabel Allende

Back Roads
Tawni O'Dell

The Bluest Eye
Toni Morrison

While I Was Gone
Sue Miller

The Poisonwood Bible
Barbara Kingsolver

Open House
Elizabeth Berg

Drowning Ruth
Christina Schwarz

House of Sand and Fog
Andre Dubus III

2001

We Were the Mulvaneys
Joyce Carol Oates

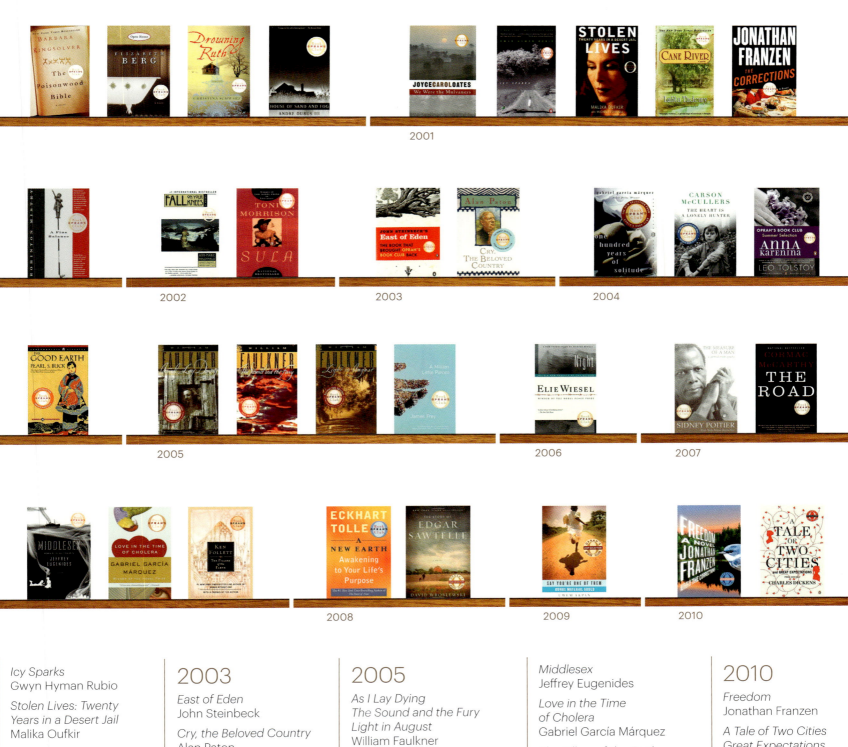

2001

2002   2003   2004

2005   2006   2007

2008   2009   2010

Icy Sparks
Gwyn Hyman Rubio

*Stolen Lives: Twenty
Years in a Desert Jail*
Malika Oufkir

Cane River
Lalita Tademy

The Corrections
Jonathan Franzen

A Fine Balance
Rohinton Mistry

2002

Fall on Your Knees
Ann-Marie MacDonald

Sula
Toni Morrison

2003

East of Eden
John Steinbeck

Cry, the Beloved Country
Alan Paton

2004

*One Hundred
Years of Solitude*
Gabriel García Márquez

*The Heart Is a
Lonely Hunter*
Carson McCullers

Anna Karenina
Leo Tolstoy

The Good Earth
Pearl S. Buck

2005

As I Lay Dying
The Sound and the Fury
Light in August
William Faulkner

A Million Little Pieces
James Frey

2006

Night
Elie Wiesel

2007

The Measure of a Man
Sidney Poitier

The Road
Cormac McCarthy

2005

Middlesex
Jeffrey Eugenides

*Love in the Time
of Cholera*
Gabriel García Márquez

The Pillars of the Earth
Ken Follett

2008

A New Earth
Eckhart Tolle

*The Story of Edgar
Sawtelle*
David Wroblewski

2009

Say You're One of Them
Uwem Akpan

2010

Freedom
Jonathan Franzen

A Tale of Two Cities
Great Expectations
Charles Dickens

Moving the Needle

"This instrument can teach, it can illuminate; yes, and it can even inspire. But it can do so only to the extent that humans are determined to use it to those ends."

–Edward R. Murrow

She achieved something that no other talk-show host, however personable or popular, accomplished before her: She became one with her audience.

Oprah Winfrey and her eponymous show have had nothing less than a seismic impact on media. Described by the Harvard Business School as "a global media presence with a definitive vision and brand," Oprah turned old media into "YOU" media. "You see it everywhere," said television critic Mary McNamara, "from the explosion of memoirs to social media to journalists sharing their own opinions and own stories. That all started with Oprah." Oprah served up an alchemical combination of confession, interview, reportage, analysis, exposé, testimony, and testimonial, all filtered through her distinctive persona. *The Oprah Winfrey Show* was never a passive experience, not for Oprah or for the people who watched her. She wanted viewers to *feel* the story, to step into someone else's shoes, to see the world from a different point of view. Oprah's goal was change, even transformation, and she achieved something that no other talk-show host, however personable or popular, accomplished before her: She became one with her audience.

The barriers came down on November 10, 1986, when *The Oprah Winfrey Show* aired an

Oprah's landmark show on sexual abuse, November 10, 1986.

episode called "Sexual Abuse: Victims and Perpetrators." "Our show today confronts a problem that is so widespread that chances [are] it is happening right in your very home, and you may not even know it," Oprah said in her introduction. "Today my guests and all of my audience members have been sexually abused, and they will tell their stories of sexual abuse and you will meet some of their molesters." Viewers were prepared to hear disturbing accounts from victims and victimizers, but they were not expecting a shocking revelation from Oprah herself: "I speak from personal experience, because I was raped by a relative," she said on camera. "At the time, he was nineteen years old. I hadn't seen or spoken to him since the day it happened, but I remember every single detail. You know, one of the hardest things in life to do is to confront your own molester. . . . And so I called him for the first time recently, and we talked about what happened twenty-three years ago. He said to me that he is happily married with a couple of children now, and didn't want to talk about what had happened twenty-three years ago. 'Besides,' he explained, 'I thought you were a teenager then.'"

Oprah reminded him what he already knew. She was only nine years old at the time.

For decades, she buried the experience in "the closet where so many sexual abuse victims and their molesters hide," ashamed and afraid that what happened was her fault. "There really is no darker secret than sexual abuse," she said. But Oprah was sharing her story for the first time because she believed "it is in the light that some of life's worst problems can be examined and solved. We're telling you today about ourselves, as so many people do on this show, so that others can come out of the shadows and get some help."

Oprah's willingness to suspend objectivity and use incidents from her own life to initiate a public dialogue—and often a healing process—"changed the nature of journalism," according to Mary McNamara. "She became part of the audience and part of the people she was interviewing. She blurred everything together." Over the years, her personal revelations included a teenage pregnancy, an affair with a married man, drug use, and food addiction. On her show, honesty began at home. She was willing to share because she wanted her stories to help others, and she expected her guests to be equally candid.

Another game-changing *Oprah* moment occurred in 1988 during the show "Skin Heads." Four arrogant young members of a white-supremacist group held court onstage, inarticulately justifying their blatantly bigoted, neo-Nazi views on race. In the audience, a rival faction of "skinheads" loudly voiced their offensive opinions. In fact, one stated that "blacks still live in the jungles of Africa," and

Mike Barrett, Dave Mazzella, Brad Robarge, and John Metzger, members of a white-supremacist group, February 4, 1988.

Phil Donahue

A Once-in-a-Century Woman

Your remarkable achievements include successes on Broadway, in the movies and in publishing. Your television show? Oh, yes, there's that. It is a blockbuster for our time, in a very competitive marketplace. I ought to know.

When our program signed on the air in 1967, we occupied a family room of soaps and game shows, and we are proud to have rearranged the furniture of daytime television. We could not have known that almost twenty years later, your program would remodel the whole house.

We've watched with awe as you have soared to a place unfamiliar to all of us who came before. If the door was left ajar for you, we're pleased to take some credit for that. We have been participants in a fabulous idea called democracy. Your program brought to the daily television audience countless worthy people and ideas that would otherwise never have seen the light of television. And by the way, just a piece of self-indulgence, our program did that too.

You have carved out a world of huge crowds, a place where your audience members get a free car. And the president calls you back! Throughout this fabulous fairyland story you have held to a noble purpose: You leave a legacy of responsible television stewardship, a program that brought light to dark places and made us laugh, often at ourselves.

There is no match for you in media history. You are not only hot; you are cool: the new Dream Girl for millions of ambitious young women whom you've inspired all over the world. You are a once-in-a-century woman.

I doff my Cubs cap to you.

told Oprah that black people—including her—were monkeys. "That's a proven fact," he said smugly. Oprah did her professional best to manage her unruly guests, who were constantly bickering and making unintelligible pronouncements, but at a certain point she gave up. The skinhead's outrageous monkey statement was an "aha" moment for her. Did she have to safeguard the free speech of extremists who had nothing significant to say?

During a commercial break, Oprah asked "Mr. Monkey Comment," as she called him, to leave, and the other skinheads followed him out. "This has been somewhat out of control," she told viewers when the show resumed. "I will tell you that in all of my years of doing this . . . I have never seen or felt such evilness and such hatred in all of my life." She realized that she had permitted the skinheads to use her show to promote their ugly ideology. "I made a decision that I was not going to use the platform for anything that I thought would not bring a little piece of light into people's lives," she resolved. At the time, television audiences were used to a steady diet of sensationalism, and she was warned that elevating the show's content would cost her viewers. "You'll lose the numbers," her affiliates predicted. *Oprah*'s ratings did dip momentarily, but she was committed to a new course of action: "Either I'm going to do what feels right for me," she said, "or I'm going to leave the business."

Vowing to separate herself from the "trash pack," a genre of talk show that specialized in stories of agony, debasement, and confrontation, she traded freak-show guests (like the skinheads) and tabloid topics for uplifting shows with positive, therapeutic, and inspiring themes designed to help her viewers realize their best lives. Not that the new, improved *Oprah* was dull or preachy. She was a modern-day Horatio Alger who understood how to deliver motivating messages through entertainment. "She really tapped into a deeply American idea of self-transformation and the power of the mind, that if we have the right attitude and positive thinking, we can transform our situation," observed Janice Peck, an expert in media and culture at the University of Colorado.

Oprah also applied her up-close-and-personal style and focus on uplift to breaking news, which she reported in her signature way. On April 19, 1995, domestic terrorists detonated a bomb in the Oklahoma City federal building, killing hundreds of people. Oprah was on the scene the very next day, sitting by the hospital bed of Brandy Ligon, the last survivor to have been pulled from the rubble. In the midst of mayhem, Oprah went straight to the heart of the story: the hope that Ligon would live, thereby enabling good to triumph over evil. As she whispered prayers to the comatose victim, her viewers prayed with her. By focusing on the human side of this, and every, news story, Oprah turned headlines into "heartprints"—indelible, emotionally charged impressions of remarkable people and life-changing events.

September 11, 2001, was the first time *The Oprah Winfrey Show* canceled a taping. Instead of proceeding with a show on fashion, Oprah and her audience watched the attack on the World Trade Center and the Pentagon on studio monitors. Subsequently, she hosted more than twenty shows on the subject, from stories about the people who were deeply affected by the tragedy—the wives and children of the victims, the heroes

Oprah cancels a taping and instead she and audience members watch live news coverage of the attacks on the World Trade Center, September 11, 2001.

who rushed in to help, the reporters who were on the scene—to discussions of war, religious and cultural differences, and national security.

In August 2005, Oprah, along with millions of viewers around the globe, watched in horror as the Hurricane Katrina catastrophe unfolded. When the crisis intensified, she felt compelled to get up and do something about it, so she gathered a group of friends and associates to accompany her to Louisiana to join in the relief effort. "Nothing I saw on television prepared me for what I experienced on the ground," she said after witnessing the devastation, the agony, the senseless suffering, and the *inhumanity* thousands of families endured. She wanted the entire nation to understand, as she understood, that there is no *them*, only *us* in Louisiana and the Gulf States. "I see the Katrina travesty as an opportunity for the rest of us to live in the space of an open heart and to show our compassion," she said.

Oprah stood behind her words. After returning from the South, she announced a monumental pledge, committing $10 million of her own money to build homes for Katrina's victims. She also launched Oprah's Angel Network Katrina Homes Registry so viewers could help "make a house a home" with furniture, picture frames, and other items that were lost in Katrina's wake. When Oprah called for people to extend themselves "in kindness and grace," they listened. In this case, she didn't just "move the needle" on the story, as media analysts like to say, she actually changed its outcome and propelled many of the storm survivors' stories toward a happy ending.

Humanitarian efforts were always important to Oprah, but she kept her distance from politics. "I've stayed away from politicians really for one main reason . . . I thought it would be really difficult to break through the wall of sound bites and what appeared to be practiced answers," she explained, and she doubted that even *she* could make that barrier disappear. She changed her mind in 2000, when the presidential race was the closest it had been in twenty years. Oprah invited Vice President Al Gore and Texas Governor George W. Bush to appear in two separate episodes.

Top: Then vice president Al Gore, September 11, 2000. **Bottom:** Then governor of Texas George W. Bush, September 19, 2000.

Both men wanted to capture votes from Oprah's enormous audience of women, but one candidate appeared more telegenic than the other. Gore, the first guest, didn't offer her a kiss when he walked onstage, which made him seem a little awkward and uncomfortable. "No kiss?" she asked, underscoring his mistake. Bush, on the other hand, gave Oprah a practiced peck, explaining disarmingly, "I'm trying to win." He was his best self that day: smooth, funny, and sincere. When Oprah asked him to name his favorite dream, he quickly raised his right hand to mime taking the Presidential Oath. "Quick!" Oprah complimented. Oprah was impartial, but the show was thought to have had a tremendous "Nixon/Kennedy debates" influence on the election. Fox news correspondent Carl Cameron called Bush's appearance a "home run." After the election, Chris Rock, clearly a Democrat, blamed Oprah for the Republican victory. "You know, you . . . you . . . you made Bush win . . . and you know you did it, too," he complained.

Oprah's first enthusiastic foray into politics took place in 2005. A young senator named Barack Obama appeared on the show several months after delivering his famous keynote address at the 2004 Democratic National Convention. He talked about his plans and dreams and won over the audience with his self-effacing charm. Since becoming a senator, he told Oprah, he noticed that "people pretend that everything that you say makes sense. Which it doesn't, right? . . . I think you [need to] have people around you who can remind you that, actually, what you just said makes no sense. . . . Fortunately, I have my wife to do that continually."

Obama's second appearance on *The Oprah Winfrey Show* in 2006, titled "Barack Obama on the Tough Questions," was more pointedly political. "If you ever would decide to run within the next five years . . . would you announce on this show?" she asked. "I don't think I could say no to you," Senator Obama answered. "Oprah, you're my girl."

The following year, Oprah publicly endorsed Obama's entry in the Democratic presidential primary. "I haven't done it in the past because . . . I didn't know anybody well enough to be able to say, 'I believe in this person,'" she told

Oprah celebrates the election of Barack Obama as president of the United States, November 5, 2008.

September 2, 2008

Top: Oprah in front of "America's Wall of Shame," which consists of pictures of child sexual-abuse victims, October 4, 2005.

Bottom: Oprah in front of a time-lapse map of online sexual-predator activity, September 15, 2008.

Larry King. She believed in Barack Obama, but she was mindful of her power over her viewers and wanted to act responsibly. She vowed not to use her show as a platform for his election. While he was campaigning, "I kept my mouth shut and supported Barack Obama as a private citizen," she said. The day after the election, however, Oprah appeared onstage joyously waving an American flag and a newspaper proclaiming victory. "I'm unleashed!" she said excitedly.

Whole essays have been written debating the "Oprah Effect" on the 2008 election. Two economists from the University of Maryland suggested that her endorsement generated a million votes for Obama in the Democratic primary. While it was difficult to measure Oprah's impact, the fact that she had an impact was undeniable. "When she steps into the world of politics, a world she has always been above, it is coming from someone that millions of people, especially women, trust and revere," observed Lester K. Spence, a political scientist at Johns Hopkins University,

Oprah refrained from expressing her personal political preferences on the show, but she never hesitated to use it as a platform for important issues. In 1991, she campaigned for legislation of the National Child Protection Act, a law that called for a national database of convicted child abusers. Andrew Vachss, an author and lawyer specializing in juvenile justice and child abuse, suggested the bill while a guest on *The Oprah Winfrey Show*, and Oprah herself became such a dedicated champion that it was informally known as the "Oprah Bill." She proudly joined President Bill Clinton at the signing ceremony on December 20, 1993.

Oprah was so committed to waging war against child abuse that she attacked it on all fronts. In 2005, she told the story of Shasta Groene, an eight-year-old girl who was kidnapped and sexually abused by Joseph Duncan, a convicted sex offender who murdered Groene's mother and two of her siblings. Groene was rescued six weeks after her abduction, and Duncan was arrested and faced three death sentences. Oprah was outraged that a sex offender with a twenty-five-year record could be out on the streets, committing new crimes against children, when he should have been locked up for life, and she expected the rest of America to be outraged, too.

Free Speech on Trial

In January 1998, **Oprah moved her show** lock, stock, and barrel to Amarillo, Texas, for six weeks while she defended her right to free speech. By day, she sat in a courtroom—she couldn't talk about that—fighting a defamation suit mounted by representatives of the beef industry, and at night, she taped twenty-nine episodes of *The Oprah Winfrey Show*, with guests such as Patrick Swayze, Garth Brooks, John Travolta, Celine Dion, Halle Berry, and other friends who came all the way to Amarillo to support their friend Oprah. The townspeople were incredibly supportive, too, Oprah discovered. One restaurant offered a meatless "burger" made of lettuce, pickles, and tomatoes in her honor. When the verdict finally came in, it was "Oprah Wins," proving that she could get a fair trial in Texas, after all. Oprah was overjoyed about her victory, but she was also happy about the lessons she learned in Texas. She experienced what she called a "bingo" moment when she realized that "everybody in the world goes through a trial in one form or another," whether it is an actual court case, a disease, a divorce, abuse, or any other difficult situation, and that you have to say, "No, I am not the devastation that has happened to me." People cannot allow their "trials" to define them. In addition to this enlightenment, Oprah came home from Texas with another gift— Dr. Phil McGraw, the straight-talking legal strategist who helped her to use her inner certitude to stand up to her accusers and win.

Top: Oprah supporter, February 27, 1998.

Right: Oprah leaves the courthouse, February 26, 1998.

Clockwise from top left: Oprah holds the local paper announcing the verdict, February 27, 1998; Oprah waves to supporters in celebration of free speech and the trial verdict, February 26, 1998; Oprah gives a press conference with lead trial lawyer Chip Babcock and legal team advisor Dr. Phil McGraw behind her, February 26, 1998.

Roger Ebert

She Wouldn't Take Nothing for Her Journey Now

To borrow a line from *Citizen Kane*, I knew Oprah before the beginning, and now I know her after the end. The final episodes of her daily show brought to a close the most phenomenal run of any talk-show host in history and rang down the curtain on the second act of a life that seems poised to have many more. What lies ahead? Her new cable network, we know. But I suspect she also has a future in high public office.

Gene Siskel and I appeared on Oprah's morning show in Baltimore. We followed a vegetarian chef. He was pureeing zucchini in his blender and made a big wave of his arm and knocked over the blender and sprayed wet zucchini all over the interview couch. That was when I saw a true television professional spring into action. Oprah grabbed the *Baltimore Sun* and gave Gene and I our own sections. Then we spread the newspaper over the zucchini. "All right, boys," Oprah said, "just sit down and act like nothing happened."

Not long after, Oprah made her historic move to Chicago. I've been watching her ever since. I would like to suggest one reason for her success. She has a deep quality of empathy. She's truly curious about the people she talks with. She sees them and feels with them. They are more than simply guests. They are people who have been through things. She cares. People sense that all over the world.

Every city had a morning interview show when she began in Chicago. She transcended the genre and became one of the most loved people on the Earth.

That's not because people were her "fans." "Fans" is the wrong word. People sensed that she was as human as they were, as vulnerable, with the same kinds of dreams. She really listens to people, and during an interview, they often feel as if she were acting in their place.

She is also a gifted interviewer, who can get away with asking the hard questions because of her unique stature. She's fearless. People understand that. I think her guests also understand that she's not out to get them. Her motive is almost always a desire to understand. That's why people open up to her about illness, crime, infidelity, shame, and their personal secrets. Her program works in a way like a confessional.

Oprah leads the way by being open about herself. We have shared her problems and admired her honesty, and we feel a lack of the self-protectiveness that many celebrities employ. Watching some of her more emotionally fraught programs, I found myself wondering, How does she endure these encounters with misery? Nathanael West's novel *Miss Lonelyhearts* is about

the author of an advice column who begins to crumble under the weight of his readers' problems. How did Oprah survive the depth of suffering of some of her guests?

I asked Oprah that once, and she told me: "I used to take in and feel everything. I could literally feel people's energy. Their nervousness, anxiety, and pain. Years ago, I complained to the executive producer about how feeling everyone's pain was making me sick. And she replied: 'Then you need to stop doing that.' So I did. I made a conscious effort to listen and not absorb the pain. Not take it on, but hear it, empathize, and let it go."

I suppose that's the only choice. She serves as an instrument for our mutual catharsis. Part of the reason she is so effective is that the show is always done in front of an audience, and its emotional reaction helps magnify and absorb. I never quite get the feeling that I'm an audience Perhaps my most unforgettable Oprah moment is the one where she was in the audience for a change. That was when Barack Obama delivered his victory speech on the night he was elected president. The camera occasionally focused on individuals in the huge crowd, and there was Oprah, weeping.

I asked her how she felt at that moment. She said, "There's a Negro spiritual, 'Wouldn't Take Nothin' for My Journey Now.' I was thinking about the journey. His and mine and the collective Ours; the sacrifices and prayers, marches, sit-ins and lynchings. I was thinking about my grandmother, who spent her whole life in acceptance of segregation and oppression, not imagining it could be any other way. I was thinking of Martin Luther King, Jr., and the countless others who dared to believe it could. I was thinking of the spiritual and emotional impact of his victory on the world."

Yes. And Oprah has had a comparable impact by her example and her standards. She helps people in ways we may have no idea of. I read some years ago that her program is hugely popular among women in Saudi Arabia, a nation where women are officially disenfranchised and more isolated, perhaps, than in any other country.

Do they watch her in English? Is the show translated? I have no idea.

Translated, probably. In a way it makes little difference. They see a proud, independent woman, in command of a situation, respected by men and women of all races and walks of life, and her very existence sends a powerful message to women in sexist and unjust societies: It need not be so. That is what her program assured us in countless different ways on many different subjects. It need not be so.

Tyler Perry, October 20, 2010.

"Today I stand before you to say, in no uncertain terms—as a matter of fact, in terms that I hope are very certain—that I have had enough," Oprah told her audience. "With every breath in my body, whatever it takes, and, most importantly, with your support, we are going to move heaven and earth to stop a sickness. . . . The children of this nation, the United States of America, are being stolen, raped, tortured, and killed by sexual predators who are walking right into your homes. How many times does it have to happen, and how many children have to be sacrificed . . . before we rise up and take to the street and say 'Enough, enough, enough!' "

Oprah implored her viewers to work with her on the Child Predator Watch List, a campaign to place accused sexual predators behind bars, once and for all. She described several known predators on the show and promised to display the FBI's "most wanted" child predators on her website. Then she announced that anyone providing information leading to the capture and arrest of one of these fugitives would share in a $100,000 reward. It was an impassioned call to action that produced dramatic results: By March 2006, five months after her announcement, four accused child molesters on the list were apprehended.

The Oprah Winfrey Show also exposed the threat of Internet predators who trafficked in pedophile pornography and searched online for potential prey. "The number of pedophiles and child pornographers online would literally blow your mind," Oprah said at the beginning of the show. "And the demand is so high for new material that the videos and photographs are getting more and more brutal, with younger and younger and younger baby victims." She described some of the horrific pornography available on the Internet, including graphic training manuals for pedophiles. On a positive note, she demonstrated revolutionary software capable of tracking child pornography and the criminals who disseminated it. The information was extremely disturbing, but essential, especially Oprah's chilling observation that "if your child is being abused, it's probably by somebody you know."

Oprah's unremitting efforts to bring stories of sexual abuse into the light, as evidenced by more than two hundred episodes focusing on the subject, culminated with three special shows in 2010. In the first, media mogul Tyler Perry revealed that, while he was growing up, he suffered brutal physical abuse at the hands of his father, and severe sexual abuse at the hands of several adults. "I'm hoping that in talking about it, that it's help-

"How many times does it have to happen, and how many children have to be sacrificed . . . before we rise up and take to the street and say 'Enough, enough, enough!'"

ing a lot of other men to be free, because there are so many of us who don't say anything," Tyler said. "The pressure lifts every time you talk, every time you are able to help someone else."

Men have suffered their experiences of sexual abuse in silence, suppressing memories of their painful pasts. To give these men a voice, and the freedom to speak out, *The Oprah Winfrey Show* hosted a landmark two-day event: "200 Adult Men Who Were Molested Come Forward." The men courageously stood together, holding photographs depicting them at the age they were when molested. Their victimizers were parents, neighbors, family friends, clergymen, teachers, coaches—the authority figures who wield power over helpless children. They assembled on Oprah's stage to begin the process of disclosure and healing. Oprah had hopes for them, and for the viewers who shared their pain. "We prayed before coming out here that those of you who are watching who have never told anybody, that you will be able to at least speak the words," she said. "Because in speaking the words, you release the shame."

Two hundred male sexual-abuse victims share their stories and photographs of themselves at the age they were molested, November 5, 2010.

Whether she was expressing outrage or approval, Oprah's impassioned on-air honesty was a defining characteristic of *The Oprah Winfrey Show* and distinguished it from other programs. Viewers felt free to disagree with Oprah, but they learned to trust that her opinions and observations were entirely her own. On the show "Dangerous Food," which aired in April 1996, Oprah offered a spontaneous reaction to a comment by Howard Lyman, a former cattle rancher turned vegetarian and executive director of the Humane Society's "Eating with Conscience" campaign. While discussing mad cow disease, Lyman told her that cows were being ground up and fed back to other cows.

"Now doesn't that concern you all a little bit right here, hearing that?" she asked. "It has just stopped me cold from eating another burger."

A group of Texas beef ranchers claimed that Oprah's words sparked a decline in prices for U.S. cattle futures, which hit a ten-year low after "Dangerous Foods" aired. They mounted a multimillion-dollar lawsuit against Oprah and her company, blaming what they described as the "Oprah Crash" on her anti-beef comments. When faced with the choice of settling the lawsuit or fighting back, Oprah decided to go to trial to defend her right to freedom of speech. In this instance, she and her fight to uphold the First Amendment became headline news.

After reading Pulitzer Prize–winning journalist Matthew D. Richtel's eye-opening *New York Times* article on the dangers of cell phones in cars, Oprah decided to use her platform to expose the reckless practice responsible for thousands of fatalities and injuries every year. The episode, titled "This Show Could Save Your Life: America's New Deadly Obsession," showed an actual road test with three drivers who boasted that they could text and operate a car at the same time, something they did routinely in their own vehicles. Shockingly, all three drivers had accidents while texting on the course.

Oprah implored, "America. I am asking all of you to give up something that you probably do several times every day. You do it out of habit. You might even be addicted to it. . . . What I'm talking about is texting and driving." A mother spoke of her young daughter, who was only fifteen pedals on her bike from being home when she was struck and killed by a driver talking on a cell phone. A widow described the day her husband was hit by a teenager who was texting. Reggie Shaw, the driver responsible for the accident, sat down with Oprah to discuss his fatal mistake. "This affects my life every day," he said remorsefully. "It's something that I can never really forgive myself for, this poor choice that I made." Shaw convinced the Utah legislature to enact some of the toughest texting and driving laws in the country, and shares his cautionary story with high school students.

Oprah launched an official campaign to turn cars into No Phone Zones, and more

Left: Jennifer Smith, founder of FocusDriven, speaks about the dangers of using a cell phone while driving, January 18, 2010.

Right: An audience member holds a No Phone Zone pledge, April 30, 2010.

Left: Billboard in Chicago created by Main Line Animal Rescue, February 2008.

Right: Lisa Ling, Bill Smith, the founder of Main Line Animal Rescue, Shrimp (also on screen), and Oprah, April 4, 2008.

than two hundred thousand people, including Jerry Seinfeld, Morgan Freeman, Tyler Perry, Mary J. Blige, Sir Elton John, and many Detroit autoworkers, signed the pledge.

An encounter with a heart-wrenching billboard and a sad event in Oprah's life prompted her to use her powerful voice on behalf of helpless animals, who could not speak for themselves. "Oprah—please do a show on puppy mills; the dogs need you!" was the compelling message Oprah saw on a billboard near her studio. She was thinking of her beloved dog, Sophie, who had passed away that month, when she asked investigative journalist Lisa Ling to accompany Bill Smith, the founder of Main Line Animal Rescue (and the man who placed the billboard in her path) on an undercover mission.

Armed with a hidden camera, they visited "commercial breeding facilities," more commonly known as puppy mills, where they encountered horrifying abuse. Many of the adorable "doggies in the window" at pet stores were the product of these reprehensible places. Ling, a veteran reporter, called the mills "a really, really scary sight" and said that she cried for days after witnessing them firsthand. The mills had to be shuttered, and homes found for the innocent dogs they victimized. Oprah said, "I am a changed woman after this show," which was dedicated to the memory of Sophie. From now on, she prom-

ised, her pets would come from shelters. She adopted Sadie, a golden cocker spaniel, and sister dogs Sunny and Lauren, from PAWS.

Kathleen Summers, manager of the Humane Society of the United States' "Puppy Mills" campaign, credited *The Oprah Winfrey Show* with being "a real turning point" for the issue. It had a huge impact on viewer awareness, helped to close hundreds of puppy mills, and enabled rescue dogs, like Sadie, Sunny, and Lauren, to find proper homes. When the dogs called for her help, Oprah listened, and she convinced others to listen, too.

Perhaps the best way to evaluate *Oprah*'s impact on media is to consider the void the show leaves after having kept the proverbial "needle" moving for twenty-five years. The silence, post-*Oprah*, is deafening *and* defining. Who will champion issues as universal as free speech, or as particular as puppy mills? Who will put a human face on disasters of epic proportions? Who will remind us that "we are all essentially the same, even as we are encouraged to celebrate our differences"? And who will unashamedly use their own darkest moments to inspire others to come out into the light? As acclaimed communication theorist Marshall McLuhan might have proposed, had he updated his pioneering study of media theory, Oprah, and Oprah alone, was both the medium and the message.

After the Storm

Oprah brought her crew inside the Reliant Astrodome in Houston to interview the Katrina survivors. As she had found in New Orleans, people were amazingly resilient and eager to get on with their lives. Hope lived, even in the midst of pain, suffering, and loss. Oprah recalled running into a young father carrying his sleeping six-year-old daughter over his shoulder. When she asked him how he was doing, he answered, "I'm gonna make it, 'cause I've already survived Katrina and now I'm just moving on love—and I ain't never felt so much love in my whole life." "You are gonna make it," Oprah answered. Love was the key to survival: the love that gave families the strength to care for each other and their beloved pets; the love that prompted strangers to reach out with money and other donations; the love that inspired prayers around the world; and the love that built Angel Lane.

Oprah called together families who had been hard hit by Hurricane Katrina and invited them to look around the room. "You might have come in with people who were strangers," she said, "but I want you to know that as of today, you will all become neighbors. . . . Every family here is getting a new Habitat home—nobody deserves it more than everybody in this room." Oprah's Angel Network was committed to building and furnishing homes on Angel Lane, and the participating families promised to dedicate three hundred hours of work to help their dream homes became a reality. Actor Matthew McConaughey made the Angel Lane children happy when he and his friends built a brand-new playground in the community. And Jon Bon Jovi and his band made a $1 million donation to Oprah's Angel Network for a new neighborhood in Houma, Louisiana. From one end of the devastated Gulf Coast to another, new communities were rising from the ashes and "moving on love."

Oprah inside the Reliant Astrodome,
Houston, Texas, September 6, 2005.

Spreading
the Love

Spreading the Love

Oprah welcomes families to Angel Lane, Houston, Texas. **Opposite, top right:** Oprah with the Franklin family in front of the plot of land that would soon be their new home, November 23, 2005. **Opposite, bottom:** Oprah hands out toolboxes to the fifty families who would be the first to move into homes on Angel Lane, November 23, 2005. **Below, top left:** Oprah surprises fifteen unsuspecting families with homes on Angel Lane, February 22, 2006. **Bottom:** Oprah with the Cloud family (Tammy, Larry, Thadeus, Ashley, and Rashad) on the porch of their new home, February 22, 2006.

The Farewell Season

"If the only prayer you ever say in your entire life is 'Thank you,' that would suffice."

–Meister Eckehart

"This show has been my life. And I love it enough to know when it's time to say good-bye."

John Travolta and Oprah Winfrey, September 13, 2010.

Opposite: Oprah surprises her studio audience on the Farewell Season Premiere with a trip to Australia, September 13, 2010.

"Oprah where the hell are you going? Why are you leaving? What's going on?" demanded comedian Chris Rock. He voiced the very questions the rest of America was thinking. Why now—why *ever*—was Oprah Winfrey ending her incredibly popular television show? "I thought it was time," Oprah answered. "Twenty-five years—it's a solid quarter-century, enough already." "No, it's not," Rock quickly retorted. "Coca-Cola don't think that way! Oh, people got enough to drink! We're not gonna give them nothing else!" But Oprah had made up her mind. As much as she loved the show, and she truly did, she was ready to move on.

"I wanted you to hear this directly from me," a tearful Oprah told her viewers on November 20, 2009, the day she announced that *The Oprah Winfrey Show* was entering its final season. "This show has been my life. And I love it enough to know when it's time to say good-bye. Twenty-five years feels right in my bones and it feels right in my spirit. It's the perfect number—the exact right time. So I hope that you will take this eighteen-month ride with me right through to the final show."

When Oprah said ride, she meant the *ultimate* ride. While devastated fans tried to

come to terms with the sad news that their favorite program was ending, Oprah and her team devised one of the most spectacular seasons in the history of *The Oprah Winfrey Show*, beginning with its launch. Assembling three hundred of her most loyal viewers in her studio, she explained that she had been racking her brain to come up with an appropriate way to commemorate the occasion. Maybe she would take the audience to New York City, she suggested. Or should she think bigger? "After all," she pointed out, "this is my twenty-fifth season. Maybe I should take all of you with me to . . . the other side of the world! *We're going to Australia!*" she shouted.

As if by magic, a plane appeared on the stage and "Captain" John Travolta, a trained pilot, stepped out. Oprah invited her "ultimate viewers," as she called them, to accompany her on the "Ultimate Australian Adventure," an eight-day trip "Down Under." Three months later, they embarked on a once-in-a-lifetime experience. They climbed the Sydney Harbor Bridge; hugged koala bears; and saw the Great Barrier Reef.

Australian celebrities, including Russell Crowe, Nicole Kidman, Keith Urban, Hugh

Clockwise from top left: Oprah onstage during a taping of *The Oprah Winfrey Show* at the iconic Sydney Opera House, January 20, 2011; Ultimate viewers petting a koala bear, January 18, 2011; A beach barbecue on Hamilton Island with Oprah, superstar Australian chef Curtis Stone, and ultimate viewers, January 18, 2011; Oprah enjoying sunset at Uluru, January 18, 2011; A twenty-one sailboat regatta around the Sydney Harbour, January 19, 2011.

Opposite: Oprah and her ultimate viewers climbed to the top of the Sydney Harbour Bridge, Sydney, Australia, January 19, 2011.

Jackman, and Olivia Newton-John, welcomed Oprah and her friends to their exotic land. Crowe, a skilled seaman, took Oprah sailing in Sydney Harbor. The trip culminated in a star-studded celebration at the Sydney Opera House, or, as guests called it that day, the "Oprah House."

Oprah also introduced her viewers to Australians who were not famous. Kristian Anderson, a husband and father of two young children, had been diagnosed with liver and bowel cancer. His wife, Rachel, was working very hard to support their family during his illness, but the strain was taking its toll. Oprah wanted the Andersons to have time for each other, and made that dream possible by partnering with Xbox to give them $250,000, money that would enable Rachel to leave her job and concentrate on making memories with her loved ones.

The Australian trip was the first of many "ultimate" moments during Oprah's Farewell Season—ultimate in the fullest sense of the word, meaning final and greatest. Back home in Chicago, perennial components of *The Oprah Winfrey Show* returned, but on a grander scale. One such staple was

The Australian trip was the first of many "ultimate" moments during Oprah's Farewell Season—ultimate in the fullest sense of the word, meaning final and greatest.

Nate Berkus and Oprah surprise Monica and Tony Jorge with a new house to be decorated by Nate, September 17, 2010.

Opposite: Before and after images of twenty ultimate viewers who took Bob Greene's twenty-years-younger challenge, April 27, 2011.

day triumphed over obesity. For most of them, new bodies meant new lives.

Oprah's "Ultimate Wildest Dreams" episode gave her a final opportunity to do what she had been doing for years on the show—make someone's wildest dream come true. Monica Jorge, the "Warrior Mom" who bravely forged ahead in life despite multiple amputations, was finding it difficult to function in the small apartment she called home because there were so many physical challenges. The kitchen was so tiny and difficult to navigate that Monica had to rely on her three-year-old child to open "childproof" cabinets. Moved by Monica's story, Oprah and her favorite design expert, Nate Berkus, joined forces to give the Jorge family the surprise of a lifetime: a brand-new home, designed and outfitted to accommodate Monica's handicaps.

The Farewell Season was also a time of remembrance and reunion. *The Oprah Winfrey Show* had a long, proud history of covering important racial and gay/lesbian/transgender issues, and its commitment to fostering enlightenment and progress was never more apparent than in the commemorative episodes, "The Oprah Show on Race in America: A 25 Year Look Back" and "Coming Out on the Oprah Show: 25 Years of Unforgettable Guests." Thanks to *Oprah*, heroes of the civil rights movement and pioneers in the struggle for sexual equality became familiar sights in millions of homes every day, promoting tolerance and change.

Oprah's amazing guests were always the heart and soul of her show, and this was particularly true during Season 25. In an historic, even monumental, "first," Oprah welcomed sitting President Barack Obama and First Lady Michelle Obama to her stage. They spoke candidly about the country's problems, expressing the hope that people on different sides of issues could find a way to work together. The president said that he believed both Republicans and Democrats shared a common goal—to improve the quality of life in America. What the parties disagreed on, he said, was how to do that. "I think it's very important to understand that we can disagree without questioning each other's intentions or patriotism," he said. "Or citizenship," Mrs. Obama added, referring to persistent questions about her husband's birth certificate.

makeovers, which enhanced women's lives by enabling them to match their outer beauty with their inner beauty. On "Turn Back the Clock—Look and Feel 20 Years Younger," Bob Greene and a team of experts challenged twenty ultimate viewers who were feeling a little "over the hill" to take prescribed steps to reverse the effects of aging. With the help of dermatologist Dr. Harold Lancer, sleep specialist Dr. Ronald Kotler, and internist Dr. Paulette Saddler, Greene led the women through a two-month program that transformed their approach to exercise, nutrition, skin care and sleep, and, ultimately, transformed *them*. In a dramatic reveal, the women walked onto the stage radiating health, contentment, and pride—and they did look younger!

Season 25 also recognized 100 ultimate viewers who each lost more than 100 pounds. Sandra, who weighed 240 pounds and hated exercise, took up ice-skating, lost 106 pounds, and competed in the U.S. Adult Figure Skating Championships in Salt Lake City, placing third in her event. Stacey Halperin, the young woman who bravely permitted *Oprah's* cameras to follow her in 1994, when she weighed 514 pounds, was back. She had lost 290 pounds and was in a promising relationship, which she had long desired. She and the other success stories on the show that

Other guests were equally amazing in their own ways. Oprah hosted a veritable constellation of stars, including the aforementioned Chris Rock, who made his twenty-sixth appearance on the show. Oprah named his routine about black women and credit cards her "number-one funniest Chris Rock moment on the show *ever.*" Tina Fey, Barbra Streisand, Rob Lowe, Jennifer Aniston, Adam Sandler, Jennifer Hudson, Diana Ross, Shirley MacLaine, and Michael Douglas were some of the celebrities who stopped by to bid Oprah a fond farewell.

During Season 25, Oprah brought back her "Most Memorable Guests," the ones who touched her heart. Peyton Kramp, now a teenager, paid tribute to her mother, Erin Kramp, whose legacy of video love letters continued to teach her daughter life's most important lessons. Kris and Daisy Green, the children who suffered through their parents' divorce, told Oprah that they still missed their mother, but knew that their father would always be there for them. "Those two brave little souls taught me about the untold damage being done to millions of children going through divorce with their parents," Oprah said. Clemantine and Claire Wamariya, the Rwandan sisters who reunited with their family on the show, came back to share happy developments in their lives. The girls were thrilled because their family had emigrated from Rwanda to America. And Clemantine, who barely spoke English when she left her homeland, was now a student at Yale.

Oprah, who called herself the "queen of reunions," welcomed the cast of *The Sound of Music,* one of the most beloved movie musicals of all time, to celebrate the forty-fifth anniversary of the film's release. Ali MacGraw and Ryan O'Neal, the stars of *Love Story,* came together to talk about the movie that made America—and the rest of the world—cry. Soap-opera legend Susan Lucci reunited with forty years worth of "husbands" from her long-running series, *All My Children.* And Oprah enjoyed a champagne toast with talk-show hosts who were her peers during her television career—Phil Donahue, Sally Jessy Raphael, Montel Williams, Ricki Lake, and Geraldo Rivera—and, interestingly, it was the very first time they had ever been together in the same studio.

Oprah brings back some of her favorite guests.

Top: Chris Rock, April 22, 2011.

Middle: Doug and Peyton Kramp, whose wife and mother, Erin, died of cancer. Seated with them is Cheryl Kramp, Doug's second wife, May 19, 2011.

Bottom: Christopher Plummer, Oprah, and Julie Andrews, October 28, 2010.

Top: Susan Lucci and her *All My Children* husbands, February 9, 2011.

Bottom: Geraldo Rivera, Ricki Lake, Phil Donahue, Oprah, Sally Jessy Raphael, and Montel Williams, November 10, 2010.

As the Farewell Season built to a climactic finish, fans and media observers fixated on one day, and one day alone—the day of the final episode. Who would be the last guest to sit in Oprah's chair?

Oprah introduces the world to Patricia, the half sister she just learned of months before, January 24, 2011.

Opposite: Whoopi Goldberg, Danny Glover, and Oprah, November 15, 2010.

She was both host and cast member when *The Color Purple* celebrated its twenty-fifth reunion on *The Oprah Winfrey Show*. Onstage with Whoopi Goldberg, Danny Glover, Margaret Avery, Rae Dawn Chong, and her fellow actors, Oprah reminisced about the film that inspired her to explore talents she didn't know she had, and to take risks. She and Whoopi Goldberg had a little reunion of their own, as they worked through a misunderstanding that sidetracked their friendship.

Season 25 occasioned two show-stopping, hold-the-presses reunions that viewers *never* expected to see on *The Oprah Winfrey Show*. James Frey, the writer at the center of the *A Million Little Pieces* media conflagration in 2006 was invited back for "Oprah's Most Memorable Guests: James Frey—Five Years After the *A Million Little Pieces* Controversy," a two-part, follow-up interview. Oprah reached out to him because she felt it was the right thing to do. Although she still believed that Frey was wrong to deceive his readers, she realized that she was driven by ego, not ethics, when she handled the situation, and said she was sorry.

Viewers were also shocked by a reunion they witnessed on the show "Breaking News: Oprah Reveals a Hidden Family Secret." With great dignity—and not a trace of sensational-ism—Oprah introduced her half sister, Patricia. Their mother, Vernita, gave birth to Patricia

when Oprah was nine and living with her father, and gave the baby up for adoption. Years later, when Patricia was searching for her birth mother, she heard Vernita discuss Oprah and her siblings on a local news show and realized there were similarities in their backgrounds. The information led her to Oprah's relatives, a DNA test, and a meeting with Oprah herself. What Oprah appreciated the most about her newfound sister was her integrity. Patricia did not try to cash in on her sister's fame.

As the Farewell Season built to a climactic finish, fans and media observers fixated on one day, and one day alone—the day of the final episode. Who would be the last guest to sit in Oprah's chair? Various celebrities were discussed, while comics speculated that no lesser a "get" than Osama bin Laden himself (who was actually deceased) would join Oprah on that momentous occasion. Ticket requests, which were at an all-time high throughout the season, skyrocketed to 1.4 million, which was more than the total number of people who had attended an *Oprah* taping in the show's entire twenty-five years.

The perplexing mystery of the last guest was further intensified by the two-part show, "Surprise, Oprah! A Farewell Spectacular." Oprah's producers planned—and pulled off—"the grandest, most spectacular surprise ever, with the help of some of the biggest

Top: Handwritten lyrics to "25 Years," written and performed by Paul Simon.

Bottom: Paul Simon surprises Oprah with a performance of "25 Years."

25 years
You are walking down a crowded street
Through various shades of people
In the summer's harshest heat
A story in your eye
Well speak,
Until your mind's at ease
25 years have come and gone
The story's still unfolding
Suitcase packed you're moving on
With the memories you're holding
Will you be home
When you arrive?
25 years
Oprah —
written with love
and admiration
Paul

If you look into your future life
Decades from this question
Do you imagine a familiar light
burning in the distance
The love that never dies
25 years have come and gone
The story's still unfolding
Suitcase packed you're moving on
With the memories you're holding
And you'll be home
When you arrive
After 25 years

You are driving down a country road
Beside a shady river
When the sky turns dark as stone
The trees begin to shiver
The Grace of God is nigh
25 years have come and gone
The story's still unfolding
Suitcase packed you're moving on
With the memories you're holding
Will you be home
When you arrive
After 25 years
25 years
25 years

stars on the planet"—a celebrity-studded tribute at Chicago's United Center. Approximately thirteen thousand people watched from the arena as the biggest names in show business, including Tom Hanks, Madonna, Beyoncé, Tom Cruise, Halle Berry, Diane Sawyer, Michael Jordan, Will Smith and Jada Pinkett Smith, and others, paid tribute to Oprah. And when the evening was over, there was literally no one left who was qualified to be the last guest on *The Oprah Winfrey Show.*

The countdown to Wednesday, May 25, 2011, the day of the final broadcast, began. Psychologists predicted that fans who were used to their daily visit with *Oprah* would experience "EOS," or "Empty Oprah Syndrome." Even actress Julia Roberts wondered how she would fill the void. Unwilling to watch alone, some people planned viewing parties at home, while others decided to go to local theaters for a communal farewell.

As the long-anticipated finale began, and Oprah stepped out onto the stage, viewers realized that they were witnessing the perfect ending. Looking back, there had been tantalizing clues along the way. When Oprah announced the final season, she said, "I certainly never could have imagined the yellow brick road of blessings that would have led me to this moment with you." That yellow brick road had led to Oprah's Oz, and she was its wizard. Now, quietly and purposefully, without bells, whistles, or dramatic giveaways, she stepped out from behind the curtain to speak about her magical journey and the importance of becoming "more of yourself." Her message to all the metaphorical Scarecrows, Tin Men, and Cowardly Lions out there was that the power they sought was always inside them. "You are responsible for the energy that you create for yourself, and you're responsible for the energy that you bring to others," she explained.

Fittingly, Oprah's last subject, and final "guest" turned out to be her audience, and for the entire show she concentrated on them. "From you whose names I will never know, I learned what love is. You and this show have been the great love of my life," she said. She spoke directly to her viewers— the 404 in the studio and the millions at home—summarizing some of the most meaningful lessons they had learned together, lessons about truth, empathy, and self-disclosure. Finally, Oprah thanked them for "being as much of a sweet inspiration for me as I've tried to be for you." Then, having completed her emotionally charged 4,561st show, she walked off the stage of *Oprah* for the very last time.

Analysts will evaluate, and probably debate, the impact of *The Oprah Winfrey Show* for years to come. At the moment, however, the true legacy of *Oprah* the show, and Oprah the woman, is best described by the people Oprah most admired: writers. Poet Maya Angelou wrote, "The universe whispered Oprah," and told her friend that her legacy was every woman who watched a show and decided to go back to school; every woman who watched and said, "Today is the last day I'm going to let somebody hit me"; every woman who watched and said, "This is the last day I'm going to ever hit my child."

Journalist Mary McNamara noted that "no sparrow was too small, or damaged, or deviant to escape Winfrey's attention. . . . Exploring and/or honoring an individual's experience of his or her life, be that person famous, infamous or just an average soccer mom, became a rock on which to build an empire and an age."

Songwriter Paul Simon composed a special ballad commemorating the tenth anniversary of *The Oprah Winfrey Show,* and updated it for the final season. "Twenty-five years have come and gone, and that story's still unfolding. Suitcase packed, you're moving on with the memories you're holding."

As Simon wisely observed, the story was *still* unfolding. Oprah's legacy is still in the making. "I won't say good-bye," she told her audience at the end of the finale. "I'll just say, until we meet again."

Surprise, Oprah! A Farewell Spectacular

"From Harpo to Hollywood, pulling off this little party" at the United Center has been, oh gosh, the best kept secret on the planet," boasted master of ceremonies Tom Hanks, as he raised the curtain on *Oprah*'s "Farewell Spectacular." Somehow, Oprah's producers managed to orchestrate the final hours leading up to the event with military precision. The biggest problem was Oprah herself. She knew that something was up, but she had no idea that a slapstick comedy was unfolding all around her. Celebrity guests were pushed through one door as she walked in another and she came this close to catching Beyoncé in rehearsal. Even Chicago's restaurateurs were involved in the cover-up, gently directing show guests to another eatery if they expected Oprah to come in for a meal.

The "little party," meanwhile, featured a galaxy of stars, including Madonna, Will Smith and Jada Pinkett Smith, Tom Cruise and Katie Holmes, Jerry Seinfeld, Halle Berry, Michael Jordan, Diane Sawyer, Tyler Perry, Jamie Foxx, Queen Latifah, Maya Angelou, and Maria Shriver, among others. Oprah's best friend, Gayle King, and best companion, Stedman Graham, were also on hand to add luster to the evening.

The musical numbers rocked the house. Aretha Franklin hit all the right notes with Oprah's favorite hymn, "Amazing Grace." Pint-size songbird Jackie Evancho started singing "Somewhere over the Rainbow," and handed it over to Patti LaBelle and Josh Groban. Jamie Foxx and Stevie Wonder surprised Oprah with "Isn't She Lovely." Beyoncé and her dancers burned up the stage with their performance of "Run the World (Girls)," and Usher brought the program to a rousing finish with the gospel classic "O Happy Day."

Was Oprah truly surprised? "Did you see my face?" she asked incredulously. Every guest—and every new moment—brought back memories and inspired another round of tears and delight. The outpouring of love and goodwill was palpable that night, on the stage and in the arena, as guests and audience members communicated their deeply held emotions regarding Oprah and her show. But the lovefest was also a celebration of Oprah's remarkable contributions to the world. From scholarships, books, and libraries for schools to the Angel Network and the Use Your Life Awards; from untold "pay it forwards" to incalculable "give-it-backs," Oprah has been a powerful force in philanthropy and, more importantly, has inspired generosity in others—accomplishments truly worth celebrating.

A star-studded surprise for Oprah at the United Center in Chicago. **Clockwise from top right:** Tom Hanks serves as host for the first episode; Oprah joins the audience; An LED tree emerges as Oprah is surprised with the news of twenty-five thousand oak trees being planted and twenty-five libraries being built in her honor; Stevie Wonder and Jamie Foxx serenade Oprah with "Isn't She Lovely."

Surprise, Oprah!
A Farewell Spectacular

Clockwise from top left:
Will Smith and Jada Pinkett Smith take the stage to host the second episode; Jerry Seinfeld surprises Oprah with a stand-up routine; Patti LaBelle and Josh Groban perform "Somewhere over the Rainbow"; Oprah viewers thank her for what she's done for them over the past twenty-five years; three ultimate viewers explain how Oprah has changed their lives.

The Men of Morehouse College

In an evening of emotionally charged surprises, one moment soared above the rest. As the lights at the United Center dimmed and Kristin Chenoweth began singing "For Good," the show-stopping song from the musical *Wicked*, tiny lights appeared in the darkness. They were candles held by men who had been recipients of the Oprah Winfrey Endowed Scholarship Fund at Morehouse College. Oprah founded the fund to educate African American men, and three hundred of those men came to Chicago to pay tribute to the woman who changed their lives. The men filed past Oprah on their way to the stage, living, breathing proof that a good deed is a powerful force in the universe. Thanks to Oprah, young men who might have lost their way to drug abuse and other desperate fates had achieved purposeful, productive lives. Now, in honor of their benefactor, they wanted to "give back." The Morehouse men pledged more than $300,000 of their own money to educate future Morehouse men.

Left: Kristin Chenoweth performs "For Good" as the Morehouse Men line the aisles and stage.

Surprise, Oprah!
A Farewell Spectacular

Clockwise from top left:
Michael Jordan joins Oprah
onstage; Beyoncé Knowles
performs her hit "Run the
World (Girls)"; Aretha
Franklin performs "Amazing
Grace"; Alicia Keys sings
"Superwoman" and
Maya Angelou recites
a poem composed for the
occasion; fans cheer as
Oprah is surprised at the
Farewell Spectacular.

Surprise, Oprah!
A Farewell Spectacular

Clockwise from top:
Tom Cruise and Oprah cheer as the next surprise comes on stage; Usher closes the show with "O Happy Day"; Oprah looks out on the audience as the Farewell Spectacular concludes; Confetti falls in the United Center; Gayle King and Maria Shriver thank Oprah for the lives she's transformed.

Sidney Poitier

A Force Among Us

Was it a generosity of spirit? Or a willingness of heart? Or were these the two forces, among a number of forces combined, that mattered most in whatever the process was that brought into being a predestined child whose life's purpose would be to touch the hearts of many millions of her fellow human beings throughout the modern world? If so, then this child's journey through life was set in motion in accordance with the laws of nature, and she answers to the name of Oprah Winfrey.

Stamina and perseverance are hard to measure sometimes, especially when called upon without even a moment's notice—with millions of eyes and ears fixed on every word, every moment, every exchange with every guest. Sometimes laughter flowed, sometimes tears. Sometimes from the guests we knew, sometimes from the guests we did not know. Yet, almost always, Oprah would connect and, gradually, she would take her guests to that private place where millions of their fellow humans would join them. Sometimes, together, they would raise the roof. Sometimes they would sit themselves down around an issue that needed to be addressed. Sometimes it was just a "girl" thing.

And so, after twenty-five years, Oprah and "the girls" have left the world in far better shape than it once was. It is now her wish to reach further, deeper, for the better self she believes will complete her life's journey. And it is my belief that, whatever the task she chooses, whatever life course she sets, there will be a work ethic, a determination, a commitment, a faith that will carry her forward day by day and set her sails with the wind at her back.

In case of fire
do not use elevators

Use stairways

Notes, Credits & Acknowledgments

In cases where guests on *The Oprah Winfrey Show* were not identified by their last name, they are referred to in the book by first name only. All dates in captions for show content refer to air dates.

Captions for Photo Essays

The Making of a Legacy

Pages 6–7: The empty *Oprah Winfrey Show* studio.
Pages 8–9: Oprah makes a call in her office after her morning workout.
Pages 10–11: Oprah says a prayer while she prepares for a taping.
Pages 12–13: Oprah reviews a script.
Pages 14–15: Oprah gets final touches before a taping.
Pages 16–17: Oprah in the control room with producers.
Pages 18–19: Oprah walks through the hallway leading to Studio 1 while others prepare for the taping.
Pages 20–21: Director Joe Terry calls camera shots in the control room.
Pages 22–23: Oprah enters Studio 1.

The End of an Era

Pages 220–221: Oprah arrives to Harpo on the last day of taping.
Pages 222–223: Stedman sits with Oprah as she gets ready for the finale.
Pages 224–225: Oprah gets last-minute adjustments from stylist Kelly Hurliman.
Pages 226–227: Oprah as she exits the elevator on her way to the studio.
Pages 228–231: Oprah taping the finale.
Pages 232–235: Harpo staff fills the halls to cheer Oprah as the finale wraps.
Pages 236–237: Oprah carries Sadie into her office.

Notes

Introduction

Page 26
"to engage in persistent, intimate questioning with the aim of obtaining a confession." Robert Feder, *Chicago Sun-Times*. April 19, 1993.

"'It's the last year [of Oprah's show], Judge,' the prosecutor explained." Don Kaplan, "Chicago Juror Hopes to Avoid Jury Via Oprah Tix," *New York Post*, April 27, 2011. http://http://www.nypost.com/p/news/national/jury_shirker_oprah_excuse_3vIQs1ux21hm2A6Kz55ibM.

Page 27
"I've always been interested in individuals..." Martha Legace, "Oprah: A Case Study Comes Alive." Harvard Business School, February 20, 2006. http://hbswk.hbs.edu/item/5214.html.

"Koehn described a male MBA student..." Ibid.

"Oprah is bigger than TV." Rob Sheffield, "The United States of Oprah," *Rolling Stone*, May 26, 2011.

A Forum for Women

Page 30
"Oprah is to women what sports is to men." Lorne Manly, "For Oprah Winfrey, Satellite Radio Is the Newest Frontier," *New York Times*, February 10, 2006.

"the way women think, talk, eat, study, shop, exercise, and lead." The Minerva Awards Tribute, "Why We Honor Her," womensconference.org. Accessed July 15, 2011.

Page 33
"I was not an everyday watcher of *Oprah*..." Lydia Grimes, "Ecso to hold defense class," www.atmoreadvance.com/2010/06/27/ecso-to-hold-defense-class. Accessed July 15, 2011.

On a woman who was carjacked. Diana Penner, "Secret 911 call helps thwart carjacking," *The Indianapolis Star* (Indiana), August 23, 2007.

Page 40
"any kind of big, successful woman has gained knowledge and insights from Oprah..." Amy S. Rosenberg, "Leaving a Void," *The Philadelphia Inquirer*, May 26, 2011.

Page 41
"the highest-rated English language program..." Katherine Zoepf, "Veiled Saudi Women Find Unlikely Role Model: Oprah," *New York Times*, September 19, 2008.

"Conversations among young women start with..." "Oprah Winfrey's Show Is Advancing Diplomacy," *San Antonio Express News*, December 17, 2005.

"Saudi women say they are drawn to Ms. Winfrey..." *New York Times*, op. cit.

"American women love Oprah Winfrey and Oprah loves them back," *U.S. News & World Report*, September 29, 1997.

"'I think I am the viewer,' she said." "Making Connections," *Chicago Tribune*, May 22, 2011.

Star Power

Page 50
"I always take the elevator downstairs by myself." Nancy Koehn, et al., "Oprah Winfrey," Harvard Business School, N2-809-068, April 17, 2009, p. 13.

Page 65
"there's no advertising power greater..." From a news story on CNBC by Carlos Quintanilla, "The Oprah Effect," video.cnbc.com/gallery/?video=1139135218. June 3, 2009. Accessed July 15, 2011.

"Interestingly, although the watch was available in gold." Harvard Business School, op. cit.

Embracing Equality

Page 88
"Nearly 70% of all Americans think homosexual behavior is sinful." Russell Chandler, "The Times Poll," *Los Angeles Times*, August 23, 1987.

"a national town hall for rational discussion about gay and lesbian issues." *The Advocate*, August 17, 1999, p. 44.

Page 90
"demystifying Islam and going past the knee-jerk pleas against discrimination." Caryn James, "A Nation Challenged: The Media; Islam and Its Adherents Ride the Publicity Wave," *New York Times*, October 6, 2001.

Giving Back

Page 111
"She believed that her role was that of a catalyst." Harvard Business School, op. cit.

In Good Health

Page 152
"In buying what we want, we hope to acquire the life we desire" Peter Walsh, *Enough Already!: Clearing Mental Clutter to Become the Best You* (New York: Free Press, 2009).

Page 153
"Watch Oprah, Get Thin," "Watch Oprah, Get Thin," *Philadelphia Inquirer, St. Louis Post-Dispatch*, September 28, 2000.

Here's to Books

Page 167
"As an editor in chief of *Publishers Weekly* noted in an interview" Nora Rawlinson in the *Los Angeles Times*, April 8, 2002.

Page 168
"a wonder, the equivalent of a course in one of the 20th century's great novels." Caryn James, "Critic's Notebook; Online Book Club as Lit 101 Fun," *New York Times*, March 12, 2004.

Page 170
"A publishing insider credited Oprah's Book Club..." In Rachel Deahl, "Bidding (an Early) Adieu to the Book Club Queen," *Publishers Weekly*, November 30, 2009.

"According to Barnes & Noble..." *The Boston Globe*, November 21, 2009.

"She's brought unparalleled excitement and attention to books." Jane Friedman in the *Chicago Tribune*, November 5, 2002.

"I still drive an old clunker of a car." *People*, December 20, 1999, p. 118.

Moving the Needle

Page 178
"a global media presence..." Harvard Business School, op. cit.

"You see it everywhere..." Mary McNamara in Emily Sohn, "How Oprah Winfrey Changed America," http://news.discovery.com/human/oprah-winfrey-changed-america-110525.html. Accessed July 15, 2011.

Page 179
"changed the nature of journalism..." Ibid.

Page 183

"I see the Katrina travesty..." "What I Know for Sure" O, The Oprah Magazine. November, 2005.

Page 184

"home run." Carl Cameron, Fox Correspondent, "Fox News Network Special Report with Brit Hume," September 19, 2000.

"I haven't done it in the past." Oprah Winfrey in an interview with Larry King, quoted by Justin Jones in "Beyond Books: Oprah Winfrey's Seal of Approval Goes Presidential," New York Times, May 7, 2007.

Page 185

"When she steps into the world of politics..." David Carr, "Oprah Puts Her Brand on the Line," New York Times, December 24, 2007.

Page 193

"we are all essentially the same." Mary McNamara, "Society Stays on Oprah's Message," Los Angeles Times, May 15, 2011.

Season 25

Page 211

"Even actress Julia Roberts..." Beverly Price, "The Oprah Winfrey Show's 'Surprise Oprah! Farewell Spectacular' Guests Revealed," http://www.accesshollywood.com/the-oprah-winfrey-shows-surprise-oprah-a-farewell-spectacular-guests-revealed-tom-hanks-tom-cruise-and_article_48151. Accessed July 15, 2011.

"Today is the last day I'm going to let somebody hit me..." TV Guide, August 30–September 12, 2010.

"no sparrow was too small, or damaged, or deviant to escape Winfrey's attention." Mary McNamara, "Society Stays on Oprah's Message," Los Angeles Times, May 15, 2011.

Credits

Page 25: "Harlem Sweeties" from The Collected Poems of Langston Hughes by Langston Hughes, edited by Arnold Rampersad with David Roessel, Associate Editor, copyright © 1994 by the Estate of Langston Hughes. Used by permission of Alfred A. Knopf, a division of Random House, Inc.

Page 116: The Nelson Mandela essay was originally printed in TIME magazine's "100 Most Influential People in the World" issue, May 14, 2007.

Page 139: "For Our World" by Mattie J.T. Stepanek © September 11, 2001. Hope Through Heartsongs (Hyperion, 2002). Just Peace: A Message of Hope (AMP, 2006).

Page 180: A slightly different version of this Phil Donahue essay originally appeared in TIME magazine's "100 Most Influential People in the World" issue, May 10, 2010.

Page 210: "25 Years" © 2010. Words and music by Paul Simon. Used with permission of the Publisher: Paul Simon Music.

All photographs throughout are © Harpo Inc. by George Burns, photographer for The Oprah Winfrey Show since 1993, with the exception of the following:

Page 6–13: © 2011 Harpo, Inc./Joe Pugliese
Page 14–15: © 2011 Harpo, Inc./Art Streiber
Page 16–19: © 2011 Harpo, Inc./Joe Pugliese
Page 20–21: © 2011 Harpo, Inc./Art Streiber
Page 24: © Patrick Fraser/Corbis Outline
Page 26 (right): © Paul Natkin
Page 33 (top and bottom): © 1991 Harpo, Inc.
Page 35: © Tom Marks
Page 39 (middle and bottom): © 1998 Harpo, Inc.
Page 41: Courtesy of MBC4
Page 43: © Andrew Macpherson/Corbis Outline
Page 45 (top): © 2010 Harpo Productions, Inc./Eric Peltier
Page 45 (bottom left): © 2010 Harpo Productions, Inc.
Page 45 (bottom right): © Kirby Bumpus
Page 46 (all images): © 2007 Harpo, Inc./Francesco Lagnese
Page 47: © Debra Falk (top left and right), © Nicolas Brown (bottom)
Page 55: © Greg Williams/AUGUST
Page 56 (top): © 2008 Harpo Productions, Inc.
Page 56 (bottom): © 2009 Harpo, Inc./Rob Howard
Page 61: © Michel Arnaud/Corbis Outline
Page 64: © 2002 Harpo, Inc.
Page 65: © 2004 Harpo, Inc.
Page 66 (top): © Brantley Gutierrez
Page 67 (top right): © 2011 Harpo, Inc./Joe Pugliese
Page 69: © Carter Smith/Art + Commerce
Page 77: © 1987 Harpo, Inc.
Page 78: © 1995 Harpo, Inc.
Page 81: © Zack Zook
Page 87: © Michele Laurita/Corbis Outline
Page 88: © Paul Natkin
Page 95: © Michele Asselin/Corbis Outline
Page 101: © Naka Nathaniel
Page 105 (top): © Heather Harris
Page 105 (bottom left): © Courtesy of Cesar Chavez Schools
Page 105 (bottom right): © Courtesy of Operation Hope
Page 109: © Kevin Davies
Page 110 (bottom): © 1989 Harpo, Inc.
Page 112–115 (all images): © 2002 Harpo, Inc./Benny Gool
Page 117: © Micheline Pelletier/Sygma/Corbis
Page 123: © Brian Bankston
Page 129: © Rich Cooper
Page 132 (top): © Gary White
Page 135: © Danny Turner/Corbis Outline
Page 139 (top left and right): © Mattie J.T. Stepanek, Courtesy of Jeni Stepanek
Page 143: © Paul Natkin
Page 145: © Reggie Casagrande
Page 146: © 1993 Harpo, Inc.
Page 147 (top left): © Tim De Frisco
Page 147 (top right): © Steve Green
Page 151: © Alessandra Petlin / AUGUST
Page 158: From the personal collection of Oprah Winfrey
Page 163: © 1997 Harpo, Inc.
Page 165: © Timothy Greenfield-Sanders / Corbis Outline

Page 170 (top left): © Libby Moore
Page 173: © Elena Seibert / Corbis Outline
Page 178: © 1986 Harpo, Inc.
Page 179: © 1988 Harpo, Inc.
Page 181: © Robin Holland / Corbis Outline
Page 189: © Erika Dufour
Page 193 (top left): Courtesy of Main Line Animal Rescue
Page 201: © 2010 Harpo, Inc./Joe Pugliese
Page 202 (bottom): © 2010 Harpo, Inc./sdpmedia.com.au
Page 203: © 2010 Harpo, Inc./James Morgan
Page 210 (top): Courtesy of Paul Simon Music
Page 213 (top left): © 2011 Harpo, Inc./Bill Smith
Page 213(bottom): © 2011 Harpo, Inc./Joe Pugliese
Page 214 (top right and middle): © 2011 Harpo, Inc./Bill Smith
Page 214 (bottom): © 2011 Harpo, Inc./Rudi Ayasse
Page 215 (top): © 2011 Harpo, Inc./Rudi Ayasse
Page 215 (middle and bottom left): © 2011 Harpo, Inc./Joe Pugliese
Page 215 (bottom right): © 2011 Harpo, Inc./Bill Smith
Page 216 (top): © 2011 Harpo, Inc./Bill Smith
Page 216 (middle left): © 2011 Harpo, Inc./Joe Pugliese
Page 216 (middle right and bottom): © 2011 Harpo, Inc./Rudi Ayasse
Page 217 (middle): © 2011 Harpo, Inc./Bill Smith
Page 217 (bottom left): © 2011 Harpo, Inc./Rudi Ayasse
Page 219: © Nigel Parry / Cpi Syndication
Page 220–229: © 2011 Harpo, Inc./Joe Pugliese
Page 232–233: © 2011 Harpo, Inc./Joe Pugliese
Page 236–237: © 2011 Harpo, Inc./Joe Pugliese

Acknowledgments

The publisher would like to thank the following people, without whom this book would not have been possible:

At Harpo, Inc., presidents Erik Logan and Sheri Salata, for their trust in Abrams to tell this important story; for their tireless and devoted efforts on behalf of this book, Lisa Halliday, Angela De Paul, and Jamie Goss Martin, with Don Halcombe, Michelle McIntyre Sznewajs, and Torie Hajdu; for their meticulous research, Charlie Smiley, Seth Zimmerman, Hilary Powell, Michelle Turcotte, and The Oprah Winfrey Show Season 25 Research Team; for graphics, Tameka Hemmons and Sara Jean Cough; and for their perseverance with legal clearances, Andreas Buchanan, Matt Greiner, Casey McMillan, Teresa Rodriguez, Carmelita Tiu, Stephanie Urcheck, and also Heather McGinley.

Author Deborah Davis, grace under pressure personified, who eloquently put this story to paper; creative consultant Kevin Kwan for his sharp eye and seemingly endless reserve of calm; Eddie Opara and Brankica "G" Harvey of Pentagram for their elegantly executed design and boundless good humor; and senior production manager Jules Thomson, managing editor David Blatty, contracts manager Tammi Guthrie, and assistant contracts manager Kristina Pereira Tully, who each dedicated themselves wholeheartedly to making this book a reality.

Editor: Deborah Aaronson
Creative Consultant: Kevin Kwan
Design: Pentagram
Production Manager: Jules Thomson

Library of Congress Cataloging-in-Publication Data

Davis, Deborah, 1952–
   The Oprah Winfrey show : reflections on an American legacy / by Deborah
Davis.
      p. cm.
   ISBN 978-1-4197-0059-0
   1. Oprah Winfrey show (Television program) 2. Winfrey, Oprah. 3.
Television personalities—United States—Biography. I. Title.
   PN1992.77.O68D38 2011
   791.4502'8092—dc23
                        2011033057

THE ART OF BOOKS SINCE 1949
115 West 18th Street
New York, NY 10011
www.abramsbooks.com